Economic Justice
and the State

Christian College Coalition Study Guides
Edited by John A. Bernbaum

Economic Justice and the State

**A Debate Between
Ronald H. Nash and
Eric H. Beversluis**

Edited by John A. Bernbaum

Baker Book House
Grand Rapids, Michigan 49506

Christian College Coalition
Washington, D.C. 20036

Chapter 1 appeared in *Christianity Today*, 23 March 1979, pp.
665–71, is copyrighted by that publication, and is used by
permission. Chapters 2 and 3 appeared in *Christian Scholar's
Review* 11 (1981–82): 330–58, are copyrighted by that
publication, and are used by permission.

All Scripture passages are quoted from the New International
Version, copyright 1978 by New York International Bible Society.

ISBN: 0–8010–0927–8

Printed in the United States of America

The Christian College Coalition, an association of more than seventy colleges,
was founded in 1976. With main offices located in Washington, D.C., the
coalition serves a vital sector of American private higher education—
regionally accredited liberal arts colleges committed both to being excellent
educational institutions and to keeping the Christian faith central to every
facet of campus life. All member colleges seek faculty and administrators
who are academically qualified, personally committed to the Christian faith,
and determined to integrate that faith into their academic disciplines and
daily lives.

The coalition brings member colleges into a cooperative relationship that
strengthens them by enabling them to achieve common goals. It has steadily
grown in membership and expanded the breadth of activities it offers to
member colleges. These schools, affiliated with nearly thirty denominations,
find enrichment in the diversity of religious traditions within the coalition, a
diversity that draws upon a core of common concern for biblical values and
truths. For further information write to:

Christian College Coalition
1776 Massachusetts Avenue, N.W.
Washington, DC 20036

Contents

Foreword

The Christian College Coalition is committed to an educational philosophy based on the belief that the Scriptures are "God-breathed" and are "useful for teaching, rebuking, correcting and training in righteousness" (2 Tim. 3:16). Because the Bible is reliable, it serves as a foundation for all dimensions of the educational program of our member colleges and universities. While Scripture is not exhaustive on every subject, it offers a basis for understanding all of reality. It is with a biblical perspective that we as evangelicals view the world around us.

The material in this volume, and in the other publications that will follow in this series, focuses on the critical connecting points that link the Bible and our various academic disciplines. The issues under discussion in this book concern the character of biblical justice, the rightful role and limits of government, and the nature of economic justice.

What does it mean for us to seek justice in our contemporary situation? What guidelines does Scripture offer us? If we desire to reflect God's character in our lives and if he is just, what does this imply for our thoughts and actions in economic life? Such questions constitute the focal point for the materials in this volume.

The principal articles offer contrasting perspectives, and each is followed by a series of study questions. The issues raised by the authors and highlighted in the study questions are then the subject of the "biblical resources for further study" that conclude this book.

The Christian College Coalition Study Guides will foster a healthy dialogue within the Christian community on important subjects rather than offer a particular "Christian solution." A full appreciation of our own fallenness and finiteness does not allow us to take the posture of having *the* solution and requires our seriously wrestling with the difficult issues of our time as faithful disciples of Jesus Christ. The apostle Paul instructs us to be "new creations" in Jesus Christ, to put off the "old" and to put on the "new"; to be "made new in the attitude of your minds" (Eph. 4:23). We understand this to mean that Christians should think and act differently because of the "light" of God's Word. This series is committed to that goal.

John R. Dellenback
President
Christian College Coalition

Washington, D.C.
June 1986

The Economics of Justice: A Conservative's View

Ronald H. Nash

A problem that threatens to divide contemporary evangelicalism is that of social justice. The evangelical debate is between parties who agree about the Christian's responsibility to aid the poor and needy. Their clash involves conflicting answers to several separate questions: What is justice? Is the Christian's undisputed obligation to demonstrate love for the needy an integral part of justice? Or is the confusion of love and justice a conceptual muddle without biblical warrant that threatens society with great mischief? Does the Christian's social responsibility obligate him, as many evangelicals are now claiming, to adopt as his means the political system commonly referred to as "liberalism"? Are liberal social programs really the most effective means to aid the poor, or are they, more often than not, counterproductive? Most evangelicals who are politically liberal believe it is impossible to be both a biblical, spiritual Christian and a political conservative.

A variety of factors complicates the social, political, and economic disagreements among contemporary evangelicals. First, few Christians, whatever their political persuasion, have made the effort to study the foundational issues that underlie the problem of justice. Basic concepts like freedom and the state are usually left unexamined, as are the details of the conflict between socialism and a market economy. Anyone wishing to deal adequately with the problem of social justice is forced either to begin with a lengthy treatise on the foundational issues or trust that the sincere reader will seek out for himself the relevant literature already available. Unfortunately, many who have attempted to present *the* evangelical view of social justice have failed to do the necessary homework.

Second, the evangelical liberals who write most frequently about social and political issues are ignorant of the major publications of mainstream conservatism. The very slogans they use against "capitalism" betray their unacquaintance with major economic works like Ludwig von Mises's *Human Action*. Other books, indispensable to any fair appraisal of contemporary conservatism, include George H. Nash's *The Conservative Intellectual Movement in America, Since 1945;* James Burnham's *Suicide of the West;* M. Stanton Evans's *Clear and Present Dangers;* and two books by the late Frank S. Meyer, *What Is Conservatism?* and *In Defense of Freedom.*[1]

Most recent evangelical publications on the subject have maintained that the demands of social justice bind the Christian to the means of political liberalism. This assertion is supplemented by allegations that because political conservatism lacks compassion for the poor and fails to support programs to alleviate poverty, hunger, and need, it is an unacceptable option for the evangelical. Previous statements of this claim raise questions about the evangelical liberal's grasp of the complex social, political, and economic foundations of justice as well as the fairness of his treatment of the conservative alternative. The argument that follows suggests that the liberal evangelical is often inattentive to important distinctions in the notion of justice, that he fails to see how his claims draw him into an unavoidable and mischievous dependence on a coercive state, that many of his programs to help the poor end up, because of his poor grasp of economics, being

1. Ludwig von Mises, *Human Action: A Treatise on Economics* (1949); George H. Nash, *The Conservative Intellectual Movement in America, Since 1945* (1976); James Burnham, *Suicide of the West: An Essay on the Meaning and Destiny of Liberalism* (1964); M. Stanton Evans, *Clear and Present Dangers: A Conservative View of America's Government* (1975); Frank S. Meyer, ed., *What Is Conservatism?* (1964); Meyer, *In Defense of Freedom: A Conservative Credo* (1962). Full bibliographical data for these volumes and all others cited in chapters 1–3 are supplied in the "Selected Bibliography" below.

self-defeating, and thus that his interpretation of Scripture's teaching about justice is confused.

What is distributive justice? Three kinds of justice have traditionally been distinguished. First, interpersonal relations involving economic exchanges raise questions of *commercial justice*. When people exchange goods and services, questions arise as to whether the exchange is fair or the compensation just. Passages of Scripture like Leviticus 19:36 and Proverbs 16:11, which oblige merchants to have just scales and weights, seem directed to this type of justice. Second, instances where some wrong must be made right under either criminal or civil law are occasions for *remedial justice*. Exodus 23:3–6 is one of several biblical passages that speak to such issues. Finally, questions about *distributive justice* arise in situations where some good or some burden is to be apportioned among human beings. Such situations are encountered frequently. Imagine, for example, a parent who must decide how to divide a pie among a large family. Or consider the case of a man who, preparing his will, must decide how to divide his estate among several prospective heirs.

The cited examples of distributive justice have certain features in common. They are *controlled situations* in the sense that they are fairly limited in size and scope. The distributors have some legitimate claim to that which they are distributing and can usually, at least in principle, obtain the relevant information needed to come to a decision. For example, the parent about to divide the pie can ask how hungry everyone is. In such controlled, everyday situations, the concept of distributive justice makes perfectly good sense. However, most of the contemporary concern about social justice pertains to situations where the benefits (like appointed offices, honors, or welfare payments) or the burdens (like taxes) are distributed by the state among the members of a huge and complex society. Many liberals also insist that the vast disparities in income and wealth that exist in a society like ours are a legitimate subject in discussions about distributive justice. A massive leap is required to get from the limited and controlled situations where considerations of distributive justice are obviously relevant to the unlimited and *spontaneous situations* found in society as a whole. In limited situations justice is possible because the distributor usually has access to the information he needs to make his decisions. But when the context becomes as broad as an entire society, no one person or central authority can ever attain sufficient knowledge about the millions of individuals and the incalculable number of decisions, actions, and exchanges that have brought them to their present holdings. The more complex a society, the less likely it is that any one person or central agency can possess all the essential information.

Furthermore, the attempt to apply distributive schemes of justice to society as a whole rests upon several misleading analogies. When the whole of society is in view, "we are not in the position of children who have been given portions of pie by someone who now makes last minute adjustments to rectify careless cutting. There is no *central* distribution, no person or group entitled to control all the resources, jointly deciding how they are to be doled out. What each person gets, he gets from others who give to him in exchange for something, or as a gift. In a free society, diverse persons control different resources, and new holdings arise out of the voluntary exchanges and actions of persons. . . . The total result is the product of many individual decisions which the different individuals involved are entitled to make."[2] The concept of social justice simply is not applicable to the consequences of a spontaneous, uncontrolled process like a free market.

Social justice, as viewed by the liberal, is possible only in a society that is controlled from the top down. There must be a central agency with the power to force people to accept the liberal's preferred pattern of distribution. And because people's normal desires will lead them to economic exchanges that will upset any original pattern, the pattern can only be preserved by the state's continuous interference with the lives of its citizens. If social justice is to have any meaning, all factors that might contribute to spontaneous deviations from the desired pattern must be eliminated.

Distributive Justice and the State

When a political liberal talks about distributive justice on a societal level, he usually has three things in mind. First, he believes the present distribution of goods and burdens is unjust because it fails to measure up to his preconceived pattern. Second, he believes the present spread must be redistributed to

2. Robert Nozick, *Anarchy, State, and Utopia* (1974), pp. 149–50.

match better his criterion. And finally, this required redistribution cannot be voluntary. Because the more privileged members of society will not willingly part with their greater share, the liberal wants the state to be authorized to take by force whatever the central authority believes necessary to meet the requirements of "justice." That this appropriation is normally effected through taxation does not alter the fact that it is an act of force.

Liberal devotees of social justice fail to recognize how their theory enslaves them to the state. They overlook the massive threat the institution of the state poses to human liberty and values. Those who profit from the power of the state have done a good job of passing the state off as a benevolent friend ready to help in every time of need. The state, they affirm, is simply an extension of our own corporate desires. But the state is not coextensive with the people. The state is the much smaller group that runs society and forces others to obey. It is an institution of coercion. The force it uses may be blatant as in the case of armies, prisons, or firing squads; or it may be applied more subtly in the form of threats. But wherever the state exists, one will also find coercion. In fact, one thing distinguishing the state from other institutions within society that use force (like the Mafia) is the total monopoly on force demanded by the state. The state cannot tolerate any competing agency of force within its territory. Because of its monopoly on the use of coercive power within its territory, the state can engage in actions that, if committed by a private citizen, would be deemed criminal. In the words of Albert Jay Nock, the state "forbids private murder, but itself organizes murder on a colossal scale. It punishes private theft, but itself lays unscrupulous hands on anything it wants. . . ." Given the state's monopoly on power and its propensity to misuse that power as an aggressor against human rights and an enslaver of human persons, one might legitimately wonder if the state has a moral right to exist.

Another attack on the moral legitimacy of the state comes from those who question the morality of the means by which the state acquires the wealth that supports its power. The vast majority of people in society acquire what wealth they have by first producing something and then exchanging voluntarily with others. This peaceful means of free exchange is the basis of our society. But there is another way of acquiring wealth: by force and violence. In this second way people who themselves do not produce anything simply appropriate whatever they can from those who have produced. Thieves acquire their wealth in this second way; so does the state. The state can exist only because it functions as a parasite on the productive segment of society. Instead of producing, it preys on those who do produce.

Questions about the legitimacy of the state are not necessarily intended to repudiate the need for social order in favor of social chaos. One result of the prevailing statism of our age is the inability of many to see how a large number of functions that have been surrendered to state control could be provided by voluntary, nonstatist institutions. However, as evil as the institution of the state may be, it is frequently a necessary evil under the conditions that prevail on this planet. The undeniable need for internal security against criminal activity and for national defense against foreign enemies cannot be met by voluntary institutions and contributions. Nor is the provision of security the only legitimate function of the state.[3] The existence of a minimal state is clearly justified. But if the powers of that minimal state are to be expanded, the burden of proof should rest on the shoulders of the statist. As Oscar Cullmann has demonstrated, that proof cannot come from the New Testament.[4]

Political liberalism, whether practiced by a secularist or by an evangelical, involves more than a commitment to certain ends like assistance to the needy. It requires advocacy of a particular means to those ends, namely, using the full force of the state to attain its goals. Christian political liberals want the state to use its vast powers of coercion to force everyone in society to help attain the Christian's ends. Is it not possible to see the spectre of the Inquisition lurking in the background? No Christian, I trust, favors compulsion in bringing people to theological commitment. But is voluntarism any less essential to social virtue?

The liberal assumes that his promotion of social justice simply means the addition of a new moral value to those known in the past. He believes this new moral value "can be fitted within the existing framework of moral rules. What is not sufficiently recognized is that in order to give this phrase [social justice] meaning a complete change of the whole character of the social order will

3. E.g., see Milton Friedman and Rose D. Friedman, *Capitalism and Freedom* (1962), p. 34.

 4. See *The State in the New Testament* (1956).

have to be effected, and that some of the values which used to govern it will have to be sacrificed." Friedrich August von Hayek, the Nobel Prize–winning economist, fears that "like most attempts to pursue an unattainable goal, the striving for it [social justice] will also produce highly undesirable consequences, and in particular lead to the destruction of the indispensable environment in which the traditional moral values alone can flourish, namely personal freedom."[5]

The necessary role of the state in all schemes of distributive justice has obvious implications for the relationship between justice and love. In fact, it should now be clear that justice and love must not be confused. By its very nature the state is an institution of coercion; it must operate through the use of force. Furthermore, if the state is to appear just, it must function impersonally. Not to act impersonally would be to discriminate among persons. Justice then can only be effected through a state which uses force dispensed impersonally in accordance with law. But this analysis of justice conflicts at every point with the nature of love. Love, by definition, must be given voluntarily; no one can be forced to love. Moreover, love always discriminates; it is always personal (directed at specific individuals). And finally, love should be willing to sacrifice, to go beyond the ordinary moral and legal requirements of a situation. A necessarily coercive state cannot serve as an instrument of love. The state's required use of force is logically incompatible with the nature and demands of love. As soon as the coercive state enters the picture, love must leave. When the evangelical liberal confuses love with justice, he is doing more than simply urging others in his society to manifest a compassionate love for the needy. He is in effect demanding that the state get out its weapons and force people to fulfill the demands of love. And how does the state do this? The state does this by becoming an institutionalized Robin Hood. The mythical Robin Hood is admired because he stole only from thieves (agents of the state). The Robin Hood–state steals primarily from innocent individuals, whose only crime is some measure of success or good fortune in life.

5. *Law, Legislation and Liberty: A New Statement of the Liberal Principles of Justice and Political Economy*, vol. 2, *The Mirage of Social Justice* (1976), p. 67.

Justice and the Market

While the necessary ally of all liberal theories of justice is the state, their avowed enemy is "capitalism." Israel M. Kirzner observes, "One of the most intriguing paradoxes surrounding modern capitalism is the hate, the fear, and the contempt with which it is commonly regarded." Capitalism is blamed for every evil in contemporary society, including its greed, materialism, and selfishness, the prevalence of fraudulent behavior, the debasement of society's tastes, the pollution of the environment, the alienation and despair within society, and the vast disparities in wealth. Even racism and sexism are treated as necessary effects of capitalism. With such an easily identifiable cause of society's ills, it is little wonder that the liberal has such an easy solution: replace capitalism with a "just economic system," a euphemism for some type of centrally controlled economy.

Perhaps the first step to any fair discussion of the economic dimensions of the problem of justice is to abandon the term *capitalism*. "As coined and circulated by Marxism, the term has retained up to the present so much of its hate-filled significance and class-struggle overtones that its usefulness for the purposes of scientific discussion has become extremely questionable. In addition, it provides us with only a very vague notion of the real essence of our economic system. Instead of promoting understanding, it merely arouses the emotions and obscures the truth."[6] We shall talk instead of the "market," by which we mean an economic system in which goods and services are exchanged voluntarily. A market economy begins by assuming a system of human rights, such as the right to make decisions and the right to hold and exchange property. The things people freely exchange on the market are things to which they must have had prior rights. The market requires a minimal state whose function is the protection of the rights that constitute the background of the market. People should be protected from fraud, misrepresentation, violence, theft, and other criminal acts.

The questions of distributive justice could never arise apart from some economic system within which scarce goods can be acquired and exchanged. The economic system produces the pie but not the criteria that determine the most just division of the

6. Wilhelm Röpke, *Economics of the Free Society* (1963), p. 259.

pie. Since economics is a value-free discipline, economic systems themselves cannot provide the criteria of a just distribution. The market does not presume to place any value on human choices. That is the task of moral philosophy and theology, which serve as indispensable helpmates for economics. The market provides incentives for people to produce and makes it possible for them to transfer and exchange their holdings. What transpires in the market will be as moral or immoral as the human beings active in the market. The moral criteria that judge those actions and their consequences must come from some discipline other than economics. Because the market itself is amoral and does not supply the moral standards to evaluate what transpires within the system, it is a mistake to confuse economic merit with moral merit. There may be good economic reasons for paying a skilled baseball player twenty times as much as a dedicated missionary, even though the missionary may be more deserving in a moral sense. Because many people are offended by the fact that someone less deserving in a moral sense is worth more economically, they believe steps should be taken to alter the situation through statist action. It is worth noting that there never seem to be enough people who are willing to alter the situation economically, for example, by paying more to hear the missionary preach than they will to watch the athlete perform.

The socialist attempt to apply moral principles to economic activities leads to a moral and economic desert. The same error is made by the evangelical liberal who wishes to replace the market, where value depends on supply and demand, with a socioeconomic system that ignores economic values and rewards moral merit. It is not difficult to organize dissatisfaction with the actual distribution of the market. It is natural to feel moral outrage at the prosperity of the wicked; it is easy to feel envy at the prosperity of the righteous. As long as some have more than others, it is natural for discontent to arise among those with less. But the liberal errs if he thinks statist intervention with the market will guarantee the primacy of moral merit. Once the distribution is placed in the hands of the state, it is highly likely that moral merit will once again be reduced to second place while the major shares go to reward political merit, as in Marxist countries. The attempt to alleviate the disparities resulting from the market's reward of economic merit could lead to a highly discriminatory and politically biased distribution that is just as much in conflict with a moral perspective. Instead of being rewarded for economic contributions or for moral merit, a person will be rewarded for service to the state.

The system of economic exchanges found in the market is analogous to a kind of game. During the course of a game, much can be done to insure that the conduct of the players will be just. The rules can be announced and enforced by impartial officials. But beyond seeing that the game is played fairly, nothing in the nature of justice permits any tinkering with the final score; nothing can be done to guarantee a "just" result, that is, a score that is morally satisfying to the spectator. One might feel that because one team has lost fifty straight times, it "deserves" to win. But any cheating on the part of the players or favoritism on the part of the umpires that would help realize the "morally preferable" outcome would be unjust. Once the rules have been agreed upon in advance of play, any violation of those rules is an injustice. And if the game is played according to the rules, no one can complain that the final score is unjust. The liberal's confusion of economic and moral merit leads him to want to "fix" the final score.

While the analogy between the market and a game serves a useful purpose, it should not be pushed too far. In the case of games, today's score seldom affects tomorrow's play. If the Cincinnati Reds beat the Dodgers 21-0 today, they both begin tomorrow's game dead even. Though regrettable, the economic game does not work that way. The economic game, in a sense, seldom ends. Often those who have lost remain losers indefinitely, and their losses may affect the ability of their offspring to play the game in the future. To be sure, proponents of the welfare state overplay this problem and ignore the countless thousands who have used the freedom and opportunity of the market to succeed in spite of great handicaps. But what if the market, in spite of the advantages it has brought to the poor of past generations, is incapable of relieving all poverty and need? Should those unable to help themselves be allowed to suffer? Of course not. Hayek, an outspoken critic of all forms of statism, insists:

> There is no reason why in a free society government should not assure to all protection against severe deprivation in the form of an assured minimum income, or a floor below which nobody need to descend. To enter into such an insurance against extreme mis-

fortune may well be in the interest of all; or it may be felt to be a clear moral duty of all to assist, within the organized community, those who cannot help themselves. So long as such a uniform minimum income is provided outside the market to all those who, for any reason, are unable to earn in the market an adequate maintenance, this need not lead to a restriction of freedom, or conflict with the Rule of Law. The problems with which we are here concerned arise only when the remuneration for services rendered is determined by authority, and the impersonal mechanism of the market which guides the direction of individual efforts is thus suspended.[7]

Similar views are expressed in Hayek's *The Constitution of Liberty*, the Friedmans' *Capitalism and Freedom*, and Röpke's *A Humane Economy*.[8] The alleviation of suffering in an affluent society can occur through extramarket means that fall far short of granting the state the added powers liberalism believes it must have. Liberal programs are necessary to the statist, not as a means of aiding the poor, but as a means to his possession of power; and power is what the liberal state is all about. "The principal beneficiaries of the money absorbed and dispensed by government are not poor blacks in ghettos or Appalachian whites or elderly pensioners receiving Social Security checks—the usual figures conjured up when social welfare spending is discussed. The major beneficiaries, instead, are the *employees of government itself*—people engaged in administering some real or imagined service to the underprivileged or, as the case may be, the overprivileged. . . . the gross effect of increased government spending is to transfer money away from relatively low income people—average taxpayers who must pay the bills—to relatively high income people—Federal functionaries who are being paid out of the taxpayer's pocket."[9] Evans's book, incidentally, is more than a documentation of these charges. It is a powerful demonstration of the counterproductiveness of liberal social policies, which always seem to do more harm than good to the people they attempt to aid. As Evans notes further, "the two

7. Hayek, *Law, Legislation and Liberty*, 2:87.
8. Friedrich August von Hayek, *The Constitution of Liberty* (1972); Milton Friedman and Rose D. Friedman, *Capitalism and Freedom* (1962); Wilhelm Röpke, *A Humane Economy: The Social Framework of the Free Market* (1960).
9. Evans, *Clear and Present Dangers*, p. 127.

19

richest counties in the United States are . . . Montgomery County, Maryland, and Fairfax County, Virginia—principal bedroom counties for Federal workers in Washington, D.C."[10] It pays to serve the poor under the aegis of the liberal state.

Justice and the Bible

The teaching of Scripture about justice is a matter of obvious concern to the Christian. Evangelical liberals have convinced themselves that with or without any support from economic and political theory, the Bible clearly commands a view of justice consistent with the values of political liberalism. Because Scripture repeatedly mentions justice in contexts that also refer to love, to helping the poor, and to providing food for the hungry, it is not difficult for them to present a superficially plausible case for their position. But these appeals to Scripture should be scrutinized very carefully. For example, some such verses refer not to distributive justice but to remedial justice. This is clearly true in the case of Exodus 23:6, which warns against depriving the poor man of justice but makes it obvious that the justice referred to is that found in a court of law. The same chapter also warns against showing partiality toward the poor in a court of law (v. 3).

Most of the confusion present in evangelical attempts to find a theory of distributive justice in the Bible results from inattention to the classical distinction between a universal and particular sense of justice. As Aristotle saw it in book 5 of his *Nicomachean Ethics*, a man can be said to be just in two quite different senses. The first of these, *universal justice*, is coextensive with the whole of righteousness, with the whole of virtue. A person is just (in the universal sense) if he possesses all the proper virtues, if he is moral, if he keeps the laws (which Aristotle thought should accord with virtuous behavior). A soldier who runs from the enemy during battle is unjust in the universal sense. So too is a husband who is unfaithful to his wife or fails to provide for his family.

This universal sense of justice appears repeatedly throughout Scripture. It is present in Genesis 6:9, where Noah is described as a just man who is perfect in all his ways. In Ezekiel 18:5 the just man is defined as one who does that which is lawful and right. Two verses later the just man is described as one who gives his

10. Ibid., pp. 127–28.

bread to the hungry and his clothing to the naked, and who obeys the laws of God. A man is just, then, in the classical universal sense if he is virtuous, if he keeps the commandments of God, if he is kind and charitable, if he provides for his family, if he helps the poor; in other words, if he manifests the virtues normally associated with a moral or righteous person. The vast majority of biblical allusions to justice appear to be examples of justice in this universal sense.[11]

Earlier a distinction was drawn between commercial, remedial, and distributive justice. Aristotle regarded all of these as species of a more particular kind of justice. In the particular sense of the word, a person is unjust if he attempts to take more than he is due, if he grasps after more than his fair share. Injustice in its particular sense arises when equals are treated unequally and also when unequals are treated equally. There is nothing egalitarian about Aristotle's formula. It clearly justifies unequal treatment in cases where people differ in significant and relevant ways, just as it mandates equal treatment for cases that are similar in significant and relevant ways. Left unstated are any criteria as to what should count as relevant bases on which similar or dissimilar treatment should be based. The man who is just in the particular sense will treat others fairly; he will give them their due; he will not be grasping and seek more than he is due. This particular sense of justice can also be found in Scripture, as when a merchant, for example, is warned to use honest weights and to treat his customers fairly (Prov. 16:11; Lev. 19:36). The particular sense of justice is also in view in Colossians 4:1, where Paul admonishes slave owners to treat their slaves justly and fairly.

The allusions to Aristotle have been entirely illustrative. They suggest a long and honored tradition that recognizes that the word *justice* can be used in several different senses. There is no reason to believe that any verse in the Bible conjoining justice with love or with aid for the needy is endorsing any twentieth-century pattern of distributive justice. Since each verse like this makes perfectly good sense as a reference to virtue or righteousness as a whole, the individual who would make these verses say more must shoulder the burden of proof. The only way the evangelical liberal can begin to find his theory of social justice

11. See Jer. 9:24, 2 Sam. 23:3, Prov. 20:7, Isa. 26:7, Ps. 82:3, Mic. 6:8, Job 29:14–17, 2 Cor. 9:8–10, etc.

in Scripture is by confusing biblical pronouncements about a universal sense of justice with the liberal's particular theory of distributive justice. Because of the nature of universal justice, it is a simple matter to find justice conjoined in Scripture with love, charity, kindness to the poor, and help for the hungry. But it is logically irresponsible to infer from these statements that God endorses the welfare state, or socialism, or any contemporary pattern of distributive justice.

I have declared my unreserved support for the view that a society with sufficient means should attempt to meet the needs of its citizens who cannot care for themselves. I have also argued that this has nothing to do with justice in its particular, distributive sense. If the evangelical liberal and I agree on the need to support the less fortunate, what difference does it make whether we call it justice or something else? It makes a great deal of difference if the attempt to pack such notions into the concept of justice leads to conflicts with other social values, supports an expansion of statist powers, encourages economic interventionism that make it less likely that future generations will produce enough to take care of their needy, and results in social action that is counterproductive and actually harmful to the less fortunate members of society.[12]

We began by asking several questions. What is justice? We have suggested the word has several functions, ranging from its use as a synonym for *righteousness* to more particular usages in which people receive their due in commercial, remedial, and controlled distributive situations. But does the phrase *social justice*, as employed by the liberal, have any meaning? That has yet to be shown. Is the Christian's undisputed obligation to demonstrate love for the needy an integral part of justice? If justice is understood in its universal sense, the answer is yes. But if justice is taken in a particular sense as applying to the spontaneous distributions found in society as a whole, this too has yet to be shown. Does the conjoining of justice and love have biblical warrant? It does only if justice is understood in its universal sense. Is the confusion of love and justice a conceptual muddle that threatens society with great mischief? It certainly looks that way. Does the Christian's social responsibility obligate him to the means of

---

12. For documentation of this point, see Evans, *Clear and Present Dangers*.

political liberalism? Based upon the liberal evangelical's failure to establish his case, we must conclude that it does not.

Study Questions

1. What are the different kinds of justice, according to Nash, and how would you distinguish between them on a practical level?
2. In Nash's judgment, why does distributive justice function only in controlled situations and not in complex, large-scale contexts?
3. What is Nash's view of the state?
4. How does Nash distinguish between the biblical concepts of love and justice?
5. According to Nash, how does a confused understanding of justice threaten a "traditional moral value" like freedom?
6. What distinctions does Nash draw between a universal sense of justice and a particular sense? Why are these distinctions so important from his point of view?

A Critique of Ronald Nash on Economic Justice and the State

Eric H. Beversluis

In a recent article ("The Economics of Justice: A Conservative's View") and book (*Freedom, Justice and the State*),[1] Ronald H. Nash argues that a Christian understanding of justice does not require extensive government involvement in the economy. As he puts it in his article: "The argument that follows suggests that the liberal evangelical is often inattentive to important distinctions in the notion of justice, that he fails to see how his claims draw him into an unavoidable and mischievous dependence on a coercive state, that many of his programs to help the poor end up, because of his poor grasp of economics, being self-defeating, and thus that his interpretation of Scripture's teaching about justice is confused."[2] It is important, I believe, to determine whether Nash's argument succeeds.

We begin with a summary of the six chapters of the book. Nash first defines *statism* and *anti-statism* as views about the proper role of the state. The extreme form of statism is totalitarianism;

---

1. The article, which appears above as chapter 1, was first published in *Christianity Today*, 23 March 1979, pp. 665–71; *Freedom, Justice and the State* (1980). Hereafter, page references in parentheses will be to the book. I shall focus almost exclusively on the book since the article was drawn from it.

2. Pp. 10–11 above.

and of anti-statism, anarchism. He adopts a "moderate anti-statism," endorsing the following definition of the minimal state by Milton Friedman:

> A government which maintained law and order, defined property rights, served as a means whereby we could modify property rights and other rules of the economic game, adjudicated disputes about the interpretation of the rules, enforced contracts, promoted competition, provided a monetary framework, engaged in activities to counter technical monopolies and to overcome neighborhood effects widely regarded as sufficiently important to justify government intervention, and which supplemented private charity and the private family in protecting the irresponsible, whether madman or child—such a government would clearly have important functions to perform.[3]

In chapter 2 Nash argues that "nothing in the nature of justice supports appeals to it as grounds for statism" (p. 77). Chapters 3 and 4 consider freedom, arguing that notions of "positive freedom" cannot be used to support statism and that a limited amount of state enforcement of private morality is justified. Chapters 5 and 6 return to economic topics. Nash repeats the old argument that socialism cannot work because it "makes economic calculation impossible" (p. 153), and he urges that a mixed economy is unstable and must eventually evolve into socialism. Finally, he considers a list of "objections to the market," namely, claims that the market is "irrational" and claims that it is "immoral." As one could have predicted, he concludes that it is neither.

With that overview of the book in mind, let us ask what a proper understanding of economic justice from a Christian (biblical) perspective implies about the role of the state. I shall take it that an economic system (i.e., a system for allocating the scarce resources and the burdens of society) is *just* (i.e., there is economic justice) to the extent that the allocation satisfies the legitimate claims of the members to the scarce resources and to a "fair share" of the burdens. So I use *economic justice* and *distributive justice* as synonyms.[4]

3. Milton Friedman and Rose D. Friedman, *Capitalism and Freedom* (1962), p. 34; quoted in Nash, *Freedom, Justice and the State*, pp. 31–32.

4. Similar definitions are found in John Arthur and William H. Shaw, eds., *Justice and Economic Distribution* (1978), p. 5; and in Norman E. Bowie and

Robert Nozick emphasizes something about the definition of distributive (economic) justice that we should note, since Nash leans heavily on his work (and cites the following passage in both book and article).

> . . . we are not in the position of children who have been given portions of pie by someone who now makes last minute adjustments to rectify careless cutting. There is no *central* distribution, no person or group entitled to control all the resources, jointly deciding how they are to be doled out. What each person gets, he gets from others who give to him in exchange for something, or as a gift. In a free society, diverse persons control different resources, and new holdings arise out of the voluntary exchanges and actions of persons. There is no more a distributing or distribution of shares than there is a distributing of mates in a society in which persons choose whom they shall marry. The total result is the product of many individual decisions which the different individuals involved are entitled to make. . . . despite the title of this chapter, it would be best to use a terminology that clearly is neutral. We shall speak of people's holdings; a principle of justice in holdings describes (part of) what justice tells us (requires) about holdings.[5]

My definition of economic justice is careful to leave open the question of which holdings are morally legitimate. It covers the collectivist notion that "society" should make all these determinations, as well as the individualistic free-market position that these matters are strictly private affairs, "capitalist acts between consenting adults."[6]

Nash's thesis is that *social* justice does not require statist involvement. I shall take it that social justice is part of economic justice, and I will argue that economic justice does require what Nash would consider "statist involvement." Nash has two arguments. One of them is addressed specifically to Christians who appeal to the Scriptures to support "liberal" policies, while the second, not specifically addressed to Christians, is based on Nozick's theory of justice.

Robert L. Simon, *The Individual and the Political Order: An Introduction to Social and Political Philosophy* (1977), p. 189.

5. *Anarchy, State, and Utopia* (1974), pp. 149–50. The chapter from which this quotation comes is titled "Distributive Justice."

6. Ibid., p. 163.

Nash's Objections to "Christian Statism"

Nash maintains that Christians who derive "statism" from biblical teachings about justice make mistakes of two sorts: either they confuse two senses of justice or they confuse justice with love.

1. The two senses of justice are those distinguished by Aristotle in book 5 of the *Nicomachean Ethics*. Sometimes, Aristotle points out, "justice" refers to the *whole* of virtue, while at other times it refers to the *specific* virtue of giving each her due. Biblical calls for justice do not mandate statist involvement in the economy, says Nash, since "the Bible also utilizes this universal sense of justice. It is present in Genesis 6:9 where Noah is described as a just man who is perfect in all his ways. In Ezekiel 18:5, the just man is defined as one who does that which is lawful and right. In fact, the vast majority of biblical allusions to justice appear to be examples of justice in the universal sense." (p. 37)[7]

But Nash is surely confused here. Suppose we grant for the sake of argument that all the biblical passages about justice refer to justice in Aristotle's universal sense. Then, as Nash says, "universal justice . . . is co-extensive with the whole of righteousness, with the whole of virtue. Distributive justice, a species of particular justice, is something quite different" (p. 75). But it is "quite different" only in the sense that a collie is something quite different from a mammal! Clearly the particular virtue of justice ("a man is just if he treats other people fairly, if he does not grasp after more than he is due," p. 38) is *part of* universal justice, just as obeying the sixth commandment of the Decalogue is part of obeying the moral law. But then if the Bible mandates universal justice, it thereby mandates its parts, including distributive (economic) justice. Surely the Bible is not saying, "Be righteous in some sense, but not necessarily in the sense of practicing economic justice"!

2. Nash says that Christians who would justify statist involvement in the economy on biblical grounds are confusing love with justice. He criticizes "the position of a growing number of theologically conservative Protestants who insist that the Christian's

---

7. In the footnote to this passage, Nash indicates what he understands by "the vast majority of biblical allusions to justice": "Jer. 9:24, 2 Sam. 23:3, Prov. 20:7, Isa. 26:7, Ps. 82:3, Mic. 6:8, Job 29:14–17, 2 Cor. 9:8–10, etc."

undisputed obligation to demonstrate love for the needy is an integral part of justice. They believe that the Christian's social responsibility obliges him to adopt Liberal statist means to aid the poor." (p. 73) Nash develops his arguments regarding the confusion of love with justice on pages 73–75:

a. The "Christian statist" is mistaken, he says, in trying to force virtue on people, since love excludes the use of force. "No Christian should favor compulsion in bringing people to theological commitment. But is voluntarism any less essential to social virtue?" (p. 73) "By its very nature, the State is an institution of coercion; it must operate through the use of force. . . . Love, by definition, must be given voluntarily; no one can be forced to love." (p. 74) But Nash himself refutes this argument in chapter 4:

> The question, can force advance morality, may be taken in two quite different senses that require two quite different responses: (1) Can people be made virtuous by forcing them to behave in certain ways? (2) Can the moral tone of a society be improved or maintained by enforcing some standards of conduct? . . . But obviously, people can do all sorts of right acts for the wrong reasons. . . . An action is morally good if the agent's motives are good. . . . But . . . there may be other reasons why people might have to be forced, viz., to perform right acts. The well-being of individuals and the preservation of social order usually depends upon people doing the right thing, whether they want to or not. (pp. 105–6)

If justice requires that people receive certain economic goods (if it is not morally permissible that they do not), then society may use force to bring about these states of affairs without there being any delusion that society is making people virtuous. It would be better if the provision were voluntary, but we may not deprive some people of their rights just so others will not be deprived of the opportunity to exercise virtue.

b. Nash states that, while justice must be "dispensed impersonally in accordance with law, . . . love always discriminates; it is always personal (directed at specific individuals)" (p. 74). But following the rule of law (acting impersonally) and acting according to love are not as logically distinct as Nash supposes. In both cases there is an impersonal element and a personal element. The impersonal element is applying a universal, a rule, to a specific case. The personal or individual element is treating people differently because they differ with respect to the criteria for applying a given law.

When the state leaves me free and locks up a convicted murderer, it is acting impersonally (applying the law without respect to who we are) but also treating individuals differently (since the murderer and I differ with respect to the criteria for applying the law, being murderers). Likewise the Samaritan who loved his neighbor did not respond in an arbitrary, ad hoc manner, but responded to the individual's situation as he did because it is a *rule* of love to bind up the wounds of the robbed and beaten. Love in the sense of *agapē* is not the special, discriminatory love one has for a spouse or best friend. Agape is love for all our neighbors, qua humans. As such it is not arbitrary but requires that I respond to specific needs and interests of my neighbor. Any neighbor with these needs and interests has a like claim on me. That is what makes agape "universal" and "impersonal."

To put it another way: To respond as a Christian to a person whose characteristics (e.g., neediness) establish a claim to that response because of a rule of love is logically the same as to respond as an agent of the state to a person whose characteristics (perhaps neediness again) establish a claim to that response under civil law. Both love and justice are impersonal and personal in the same ways. They differ in that the characteristics that call forth a response and the response called forth differ. But they are not incompatible: a certain type of civil law may be one of the things required by love.

c. Nash suggests two further arguments, but they are even weaker. According to the first, "love should be willing to sacrifice, to go beyond the ordinary moral and legal requirements of a situation. A necessarily coercive State cannot serve as an instrument of love." (p. 74) One can agree with Nash that love should be willing to go beyond the ordinary moral requirements of a situation. But his conclusion does not follow, for anyone committed to love is committed, at a minimum, to the ordinary moral requirements. And if the ordinary moral requirements are that certain economic rights be respected, then how is it a confusion of love with justice to ensure that they be respected?

Finally, Nash suggests that state taxation for "economic justice" is really theft:

> As soon as the coercive State enters the picture, love must leave. When the Christian statist confuses love with justice, he is doing

more than simply urging others in his society to manifest a compassionate love for the needy. He is in effect demanding that the State get out its weapons and force people to fulfill the demands of love. And how does the State do this? The State does this by becoming an institutionalized Robin Hood. The mythical Robin Hood is admired because he only stole from thieves (agents of the State). The Robin Hood State steals primarily from innocent individuals whose only crime was some measure of success or good fortune in life. (p. 74)

But Nash gives no arguments that taxation is theft. Such arguments as he thinks he has must be related to his use of Nozick's philosophy, which we examine below.

A Biblical View of Economic Justice

Nash's list of biblical statements regarding justice (above, n. 7) is curiously selective. While this is not the place for a full treatment of biblical teachings regarding economic justice, it is worth considering some of the biblical passages that should shape a more adequate Christian view of economic justice.[8]

Ezekiel 34:16b–24 is an important passage overlooked by Nash. It explicitly indicates God's condemnation of societies that tolerate poverty alongside plenty ("I myself will judge between the fat sheep and the lean sheep"); it indicates environmental obligations (condemning trampling the grass and muddying the water); and it shows the duty of the state to provide economic justice (God will bring about justice through his shepherd-*prince* David).

> I will bind up the injured and strengthen the weak, but the sleek and the strong I will destroy. I will shepherd the flock with justice.
> . . . I will judge between one sheep and another, and between rams and goats. Is it not enough for you to feed on the good pasture? Must you also trample the rest of your pasture with your feet? Is it not enough for you to drink clear water? Must you also muddy the rest with your feet? Must my flock feed on what you have trampled and drink what you have muddied with your feet?
> . . . See, I myself will judge between the fat sheep and the lean

8. For the material of this section I follow the unpublished paper "Biblical Principles and Economic Theory" prepared by my colleague George N. Monsma for the conference entitled "International Economics and the Bible: A Dialogue," held at Bel Air Presbyterian Church, Los Angeles, October 23–27, 1980.

sheep. Because you shove with flank and shoulder, butting all the weak sheep with your horns until you have driven them away, I will save my flock, and they will no longer be plundered. I will judge between one sheep and another. I will place over them one shepherd, my servant David, and he will tend them; he will tend them and be their shepherd. I the Lord will be their God, and my servant David will be prince among them. I the Lord have spoken.

Exodus 22:26–27 also speaks about economic justice: "If you take your neighbor's cloak as a pledge, return it to him by sunset, because his cloak is the only covering he has for his body. What else will he sleep in? When he cries out to me, I will hear, for I am compassionate." The give-and-take of economic life ("[shoving] with flank and shoulder, butting all the weak sheep . . . until you have driven them away") may not deprive people of certain fundamental goods such as a cloak to sleep in at night. A person has a right to the material goods she or he needs for a decent existence. Thus the Bible teaches that there are rights to specific kinds of economic goods, and that these rights bind governments as well as individuals. One final passage indicates again the responsibility of the king (the state):

> "Does it make you a king
>   to have more and more cedar?
> Did not your father have food and drink?
>   He did what was right and just,
>   so all went well with him.
> He defended the cause of the poor and needy,
>   and so all went well.
> Is that not what it means to know me?"
>   declares the Lord. (Jer. 22:15–16)

Since the cause of the poor and needy includes more than juridical fairness (we have seen that they have specific economic rights), economic justice is the legitimate concern of the state as well as of private individuals.

These biblical passages and many more provide the basis for the following set of principles, which George N. Monsma has derived from his biblical studies:

a. Those who have been entrusted with resources have only a limited right to the personal use of them or the goods they can produce.

b. Those who have been entrusted with resources have a duty to use them productively in order to meet their own families' needs and to meet the needs of others who do not have enough to meet their own needs.

c. Societies have a duty to provide just structures (including systems of property rights). For structures to be just they must at least:

    i. assure all families access to the basic necessities of life at all times;

    ii. provide all families with the opportunity to develop and use their God-given talents and other resources in such a way that they can provide for their own needs, at least in the long run;

    iii. provide all families with the economic freedom necessary to enable them to exercise responsible economic stewardship of their resources, at least in the long run (this includes having decision-making opportunities in the use of their resources in production as well as in consumption);

    iv. place limits on the concentration of wealth, income, and economic power in the society (for this is necessary in order to achieve the first three).

d. Individuals and societies must care for their natural environment and not exhaust its resources to such an extent that future generations lack the possibility of providing all with the things listed above in c.[9]

If society is to satisfy these standards, the state will have to be involved. As we will see below, the free market will not suffice.

Nash, Nozick, and Economic Justice

Following Nozick, Nash views economic justice not in terms of patterns or end-states but in terms of historical processes that generate "entitlements." On a "pattern view" of justice, a system is just if it results in the right pattern of holdings (e.g., a pattern of equality or of holdings in proportion to need). An "end-result" view finds justice in social arrangements that contribute to some desired end (e.g., the greatest good of the greatest number). Nash follows Nozick in holding that pattern or end-state views apply only in situations that are "limited" and "controlled" and in

9. Monsma, "Biblical Principles and Economic Theory," pp. 10–11.

which distributors themselves have the right to distribute.[10] He offers three arguments: (1) In society as a whole, no one has sufficient relevant information to attempt to achieve the desired pattern of distribution. (2) ". . . no central authority really has a right to the things it usually distributes." (3) To maintain any pattern would violate the freedom of individuals to engage in capitalistic acts among consenting adults, since individual differences in effort, ability, and taste would soon disrupt the pattern. Some would work more and play less than others. Some would save and invest while others would consume. Some would give gifts that others would receive. (pp. 49–50)

These arguments are not equally good. First, it is only partly true that in society as a whole there is no one with sufficient information. If justice requires control not of the whole pattern but only of key aspects (e.g., ensuring minimum income to all), then surely an effectively decentralized bureaucracy *could* have the right knowledge.

The second argument, that no central authority has the *right* to the things it distributes, presupposes a specific view of property rights that seems inconsistent with the Christian view of stewardship rights presented above. If individuals have specific economic rights (to possess certain goods), then the property rights of others (the nature of their entitlements) are constrained by those rights, and taxation to ensure those rights does not violate the rights of the taxed.

Nash's third argument does, I think, support an historical-entitlement view of economic justice. Most Christians would agree that individuals should be free to buy and sell, to hire out their labor, to save and invest, and to give gifts. (This would be an obvious way to enable people to exercise the responsible economic stewardship that Monsma's analysis calls for.) If so, then the difficulties with pattern and end-state views that Nash points out are real. Any pattern that we might establish would very quickly be destroyed.[11] To maintain a desired pattern of holdings,

10. For example, says Nash, in distributing medical care. Presumably he has in mind something like a private charity hospital, since he opposes state control of medical services.

11. Nozick uses the example of someone like Wilt Chamberlain. Assume that everyone had equal income for a given period. Then let Chamberlain offer to play basketball to entertain people if they will each pay him $1 per night. Suppose that

either the state would have to control all economic transactions or occasionally it would have to step in to reestablish the pattern. Nash emphasizes the apparent moral difficulty of the latter option: ". . . at the time of each redistribution, people who had acquired holdings honestly and fairly would be deprived of them without recourse; and this would be done in the name of justice" (p. 51). Of course that is precisely what the Book of Leviticus envisions happening in the year of Jubilee. But I think the jubilee idea can fit into a proper entitlement view and does not require that our basic conception of justice in holdings be in terms of pattern or end-state criteria.

If individuals should have the right to engage in free economic exchanges, and if society should not try in general to constrain the nature of those exchanges in order to achieve some overall pattern or end-result, how then is the problem of who gets what in society to be solved? "Laissez-nous faire," says Nash. Let the free market take care of the distribution. But are there not all kinds of flaws in the market? Will the market guarantee people's economic rights?

Nash recognizes that there will be needy people in a market economy and that society should not let them starve: "But what if the market, in spite of the advantages it has brought to the poor of past generations, is incapable of relieving all poverty and need? Should those unable to help themselves be allowed to suffer? Of course not." (p. 57) He follows Hayek in proposing an "assured minimum income" but claims that "the alleviation of suffering in an affluent society can occur through extra-market means that fall far short of granting the State the added powers statists believe it must have" (p. 57). Any such program would be charity, however, not justice: "I have already declared my support for the view that a society with sufficient means should attempt to meet the needs of its citizens who cannot care for themselves. I have also argued that this has nothing to do with justice in its par-

---

over the course of the season, 200,000 people come to see him play. Then, whereas before he started entertaining, everyone (including the ordinary professional ball players) earned $10,000, in the new scenario the equality-pattern is broken because of the voluntary exchanges between Chamberlain and 200,000 people. Unless we rule out such voluntary exchanges, Nash and Nozick argue, we could never *maintain* a desired pattern even if we once established it.

ticular, distributive sense (social justice)." (p. 76)[12] Thus for Nash, with the exception of the minimum assured income provided to those who cannot "make it" in the market, the cause of economic justice is best served by a free market and a minimal state: "If a person is entitled to his holdings because its original acquisition was just and because the subsequent transfers that led to his holdings were just, then he and others like him are entitled to their holdings and the distribution is just regardless of its pattern" (pp. 47–48).

A Critique of Nash's Version of Nozick

Though an historical-entitlement approach to issues of economic justice seems correct, Nash makes serious errors in his use of Nozickean analysis, errors we must now identify.

1. Nash indicates in the previous quotation the conditions for a just distribution: (i) the original acquisition of a holding and (ii) all subsequent transfers that led to the present pattern of holdings must have been just. The two conditions are not only sufficient but necessary, however, and Nash's failure to recognize this leads him to ignore one-third of Nozick's theory of economic justice, "justice in rectification."

Justice in rectification is needed because many people's holdings either were not acquired by legitimate means (of original acquisition or of transfer) or were acquired from people who originally acquired them in illegitimate ways. Carl Sandburg illustrates the point:

> "Get off this estate."
> "What for?"
> "Because it's mine."

12. This position (which follows Friedman and Hayek) hardly seems compatible with Nash's absolutist view of private property. How will the assured minimal income be provided without having a "Robin Hood–State"? Nash wrote: "Because the more privileged members of society will not willingly part with their greater share, the Liberal wants the State to be authorized to take by force whatever the central authority believes necessary to meet the requirements of 'justice.' That this appropriation is normally effected through taxation does not, of course, alter the fact that it is an act of force." (p. 47) The redistribution is, of course, no more legitimate—on Nash's principles—for being called "charity" rather than "justice."

"Where did you get it?"
"From my father."
"Where did he get it?"
"From his father."
"And where did he get it?"
"He fought for it."
"Well, I'll fight you for it."[13]

Much of today's inequality of wealth, if we could trace it back, would be found to be based on what Karl Marx called the "primitive capitalist accumulation" of the early modern period, on the violent, monopolistic, often dishonest and illegal activities of the late–nineteenth-century "robber barons," and on the three hundred years of slavery that still affect the relative positions of blacks and whites.

For Nozick there are three parts to an entitlement theory of justice: principles of justice in original acquisition, principles of justice in transfer, and principles of justice in the rectification of previous injustices. Nozick points out the potentially large role that the state might have to play in bringing about justice in rectification: if these principles of justice in acquisition and justice in transfer are violated, "the principle of rectification comes into play." How important is this concern with rectification? Cannot the courts of law handle it in the normal course of affairs? Not if my examples above carry weight. For they suggest that perfectly "legal" holdings may be unjust. Nozick writes:

Perhaps it is best to view some patterned principles of distributive justice as rough rules of thumb meant to approximate the general results of applying the principle of rectification of injustice. For example, lacking much historical information, and assuming (1) that victims of injustice generally do worse than they otherwise would and (2) that those from the least well-off group in the society have the highest probabilities of being the (descendants of) victims of the most serious injustice who are owed compensation by those who benefited from the injustices (assumed to be those better off, though sometimes the perpetrators will be others in the worst-off group), then a *rough* rule of thumb for rectifying injustices might seem to be the following: organize society so as to

13. *The People, Yes* (New York: Harcourt, Brace & World, 1936), p. 75; quoted in Virginia Held, ed., *Property, Profits, and Economic Justice* (1980), p. ii.

maximize the position of whatever group ends up least well-off in the society. This particular example may well be implausible, but an important question for each society will be the following: given *its* particular history, what operable rule of thumb best approximates the results of a detailed application in that society of the principle of rectification?

Nozick does not try to answer this question in his book, but he indicates its significance:

> These issues are very complex and are best left to a full treatment of the principle of rectification. In the absence of such a treatment applied to a particular society, one *cannot* use the analysis and theory presented here to condemn any particular scheme of transfer payments, unless it is clear that no considerations of rectification of injustice could apply to justify it. Although to introduce socialism as the punishment for our sins would be to go too far, past injustices might be so great as to make necessary in the short run a more extensive state in order to rectify them.[14]

Why does Nash disregard Nozick's warning that "one *cannot* use the analysis and theory presented here to condemn any particular scheme of transfer payments, unless it is clear that no considerations of rectification of injustice could apply to justify it?"

2. Not only does Nash ignore justice in rectification, he fails to explain what principles determine justice in original acquisition and justice in transfer. Based on his repeated claim that there is no role for the state in bringing about social justice, I conclude that Nash does not perceive significant economic injustice in our societal structure today. One wonders if Nash has ever contemplated the workings of the free-market economy from the perspective of the people in John Steinbeck's *The Grapes of Wrath*. Our examination of biblical teachings on justice also shows that the Christian cannot be as sanguine as Nash seems to be about economic justice. Application of the ideas of stewardship and property rights as developed by Monsma suggests that in our society holdings are not based on proper principles of justice in original acquisition and justice in transfer. It is even less likely

14. *Anarchy, State, and Utopia* (1974), pp. 230–31.

that a laissez-faire economy would satisfy those norms. I invite Nash to join other Christians in an open-minded effort to define, in the light of special and general revelation, the correct principles of justice in original acquisition, justice in transfer, and justice in rectification. Better understanding than we now have is necessary before Christians can speak responsibly to public policy.

Where the Market Fails

Throughout the book Nash clearly assumes that voluntary market exchange of goods and services is both necessary and sufficient for justice in transfer. But, as I have suggested, *The Grapes of Wrath* serves as an extensive and detailed case study of how the free market fails to provide justice in transfer. It also shows how the "minimal" state is not "neutral" but supports the vested interests of the rich and propertied, most of whom no doubt are sincere anti-statists. Note that the Joads did at one time own land and did have access to the means of living a productive life, but that they were dispossessed through the legal and natural operations of the market economy (first borrowing because of crop failure, then falling into sharecropping as more hard times followed, finally being put off the land as mechanization and large-scale farming took over). Why does the market, left to itself, tend to generate economic injustice?[15]

1. Nash seems to assume, mistakenly, that there is some universal form of property rights that the minimal state could easily recognize (through the thought experiment of "state-of-nature political philosophy") and define in law. But while there is a natural right to property, the form this right takes depends on the society and conditions. Society, state, and the specification of

15. The analysis here follows standard economics texts, though they focus on "efficiency" breakdowns rather than on problems of economic justice. See Walter Nicholson, *Microeconomic Theory: Basic Principles and Extensions*, 2d ed. (1978); and Robin W. Boadway, *Public Sector Economics* (1979). In "Biblical Principles" Monsma explores the difficulties from the Christian perspective with the concepts of economic efficiency and Pareto optimality. We can explore how "market failures" lead to injustice without assuming that in the absence of such failures, some desirable condition of Pareto optimality would result.

property rights are coeval.[16] There is no specific right to property apart from the society and some (perhaps primitive) state. Likewise not all the forms that legal property rights can take will satisfy God's norms of economic justice. The "market" cannot solve the problem of what form property rights should take; it *assumes* a solution. Much of Nash's rejection of "statism" is really a rejection of efforts to redefine property rights in what are taken to be more just ways.

2. The economists' model of a perfectly competitive market differs in crucial and well-known ways from the real-world market economy. These "market failures" not only affect the efficiency of markets, but also can lead to exchanges and production that are not just. If certain stringent conditions are satisfied, the "market" yields an "efficient" production and allocation of resources. Likewise, under these conditions, if there is some *initially just distribution* of ownership of resources, then the market assures justice in transfer among rational, adult agents. Unfortunately these stringent conditions do not exist in the real world. This and the following items spell out some of the ways in which "free-market exchange" can involve economic injustice.

In a dynamic, evolving economy with continuous overlap of generations, it is not very easy to make sense of the idea of "initial ownership of resources being justly distributed."[17] Most economic models ignore the overlap of generations, the continual entry into society of new citizens. Likewise most "entitlement" views of economic justice ignore the complication that "generations" present for speaking of "justice in original acquisition." Certainly Nash does not consider what "birthright" a newborn child has. What is justice in original acquisition for a newborn child, arriving late on the scene? A laissez-faire approach to bequests and inheritances will not ensure that each newborn child receives the birthright that God intends for him or her. Some form of governmental transfer, at least to the very poor of the new generation, seems called for.

16. On the historical contingency of the capitalist form of property, see Karl Polanyi, *The Great Transformation* (1944); and Robert L. Heilbroner, *The Making of Economic Society*, 6th ed. (1980).

17. See David Gauthier, "Economic Rationality and Moral Constraints," in Peter A. French, Theodore E. Uehling, Jr., and Howard K. Wettstein, eds., *Studies in Ethical Theory*, Midwest Studies in Philosophy, vol. 3 (1978), pp. 75–96.

3. "Perfect competition" assumes that all buyers and sellers are "price takers," that is, that there is no monopoly behavior. But in the real world nearly everyone, from baseball owners and players dickering over the spoils of their monopoly to the American Medical Association limiting enrollment in medical schools to keep up the price of medical service, seems eager and able to gain advantage from market power. The Christian must ask when and where the exercise of monopolistic power results in distributive injustices and what the appropriate response is.

While Nash believes that "a clear and defensible definition of *monopoly*" cannot be given (p. 185), that is untrue. *Monopoly* here refers to "possessing market power"; a firm or individual has market power when, faced with a downward-sloping demand curve, it can choose to make different quantities available at different prices.

Capitalistic acts between consenting adults may not result in justice in transfer if there is monopoly power on one side. Often one person gives another an "offer he cannot turn down." If I am starving and destitute and you have plenty, you can extort virtually any concession from me in exchange for some food. But such an exchange is not necessarily just, especially if my need and dependency are the result of your monopsony position in the labor market.[18] In the words of a familiar folksong:

> Saint Peter, don't you call me 'cause I can't go.
> I owe my soul to the company store.

Nash responds at this point that voluntary exchanges occur only if both parties believe that they will benefit from them: "Whether the exchange really was mutually beneficial is beside the point; it took place because both sides believed it was beneficial. As long as force and fraud are excluded from economic exchange, both parties can walk away as winners." (p. 169) How are we to understand force and fraud, though? If you know something that would change my readiness to exchange but you do not tell me of it, is that not "fraud"? If you employ me for starvation

---

18. *Monopsony* is market power on the buying or hiring side. A monopsonist is the only (or, in our looser language, one of the few) buyer of a product or employer of labor.

wages because there is no other job for me, is that not "force"? Nash points out that "the market is a tool that is used by both moral and immoral people." He continues: "It hardly seems fair to blame it [the market] for the immoral practices of some without also praising it for the indispensable service it affords to moral people" (p. 169).

Nash forgets that once we have handed out the appropriate praise and blame, we also need to do what we can to protect those who otherwise would be victimized by the immoral users of the market.

Nash also holds that the monopolies that supposedly make such extortion possible themselves can only exist because of government patronage:

> It is impossible for the market to generate monopolies. Monopolies result from two other causes: (1) the human propensity to escape the uncertainty of the market; and (2) the existence of the only organization powerful enough to permit monopolies to exist, namely, the State. Historically, it is impossible to point to any single monopoly that did not arise as a result of special favors from government. The way to terminate monopolies is for the State to end its practice of dispensing privileged treatment. (p. 130)

There is surely much truth in what Nash says. But he should take his analysis a step further, since special privileges will continue as long as a democratic government is susceptible to the influence of special-interest groups.[19] Perhaps the most just response is to work to mitigate the unjust effects of monopoly, wherever it arises.

While many monopolies arise from state favor, not all do. Economies of scale often lead naturally to monopoly. (Even Friedman in his list of state functions recognizes the existence of "tech-

19. See William Greider, "The Education of David Stockman," *The Atlantic Monthly* 248 (December 1981): 27–40, 43–47, 50–54. While Nash treats the "State" as a self-contained entity doing its own pleasure, it is much more reasonable to think of it as doing the pleasure of the people or of parts of the people. Nash's book lacks any sense of government as a process in which the people of a society try to get what they want. While *1984* is a valuable book to read and contemplate, it does not describe what actually happens in capitalist democracies.

nical monopolies" that need to be "countered.") These need not be large-scale industries such as energy or auto manufacturing. The small town that can support only one general store generates a monopoly. Furthermore there are often good reasons for the state to create monopolies. Friedman notwithstanding, it would be foolish to trust the "market" to sort out the good and bad physicians. Thus the market will include many kinds of monopolies, and each may require, for economic justice, some form of state control of pricing and output to prevent the monopolists from getting more than their fair share.[20]

4. The problem of *knowledge* in real-world economies can also lead to injustice. "Perfect competition" assumes that people have complete knowledge about products. In the real world such knowledge is often not available or is prohibitively expensive or is a "public good" (discussed below) that the market will fail to provide. Economic injustice can occur when one party to an exchange takes advantage of the other's unavoidable ignorance. For this reason we have strict "inside information" laws governing dealings on the stock market, though most other transactions cannot be so closely monitored. Nash agrees that market exchanges are just only if free from fraud. At what degree of "unequal information" does fraud occur? Can society arrange the rules of property to compensate for unavoidable "fraud" that will go on? Obviously justice does not require that the state provide any and all information that citizens might need. But where lack of knowledge that the state can provide causes seriously unjust distribution of economic goods, we should not accept laissez faire.

5. Many economic goods by their very nature will not be produced in appropriate quantities by the free market, for example, the police and military protection beloved by the minimalist. These goods are "public goods," characterized in varying degrees by "nonrival consumption" and "nonexcludability." A good is characterized by nonrival consumption if, once it is produced or made available, some large group can consume or use it without one individual's consumption being limited by the next person's. National defense is "consumed" by everyone in society, and an

---

20. Nash presents additional arguments for rejecting the "monopoly problem." Space does not permit further rebuttal here.

increase in the population does not reduce anyone's consumption of it or increase its cost (the marginal cost of one more user is zero). Many goods characterized by nonrival consumption are also "nonexcludable." This means that it is impossible or prohibitively costly to exclude people from the consumption or use of the good (if, say, they refuse to pay for it). National defense is a good example of a good that is nonexcludable, while bus rides are excludable.

Suppose that, in the absence of a government, everyone were to get together and decide that it would be good to have an army and a navy. Unfortunately the project would never get off the ground, since everyone would reason as follows: "I will be equally protected by the national defense force whether or not I pay for it (because of nonexcludability and nonrival consumption), so why should I pay for it? Let the others pay." Thus everyone would try to be a "free rider," and the "market" would fail to provide the desired good.

If such public goods are to be provided at all, they must be provided by the government, since only the government can enforce payment by all. If some of these public goods are such that certain or all people have a *right* to them, then for the state not to provide them is economic injustice. Thus Christians should ask which public goods individuals have a right to. It seems likely that the list will extend far beyond police protection and national defense to include fire protection, highways, public health (sanitation, controls on the spread of communicable diseases, etc.), and knowledge of who is a competent physician.

Nash accepts public goods, though he does not resolve the conflict between having the government finance them and the "Robin Hood–State" such financing implies. Instead he plays down their importance. Thus he ends up differing from the "liberals" only on nonprincipial matters, calling for more *private production* of government-financed public goods and maintaining that society makes *too many* public goods and spreads the cost of supporting them far beyond those who benefit. To differ from statists only in the judgment of relative costs and benefits is a far cry from the principial anti-statism that Nash started with. It significantly changes the nature of the argument.

6. An economic externality, which is another source of market failure, arises when a basically private activity has certain "spillover" costs or benefits to other people that are not included

in the costs and benefits considered by the agents. Recent economic analysis has shown a wide range of economic questions, in addition to pollution, to which the price system does not give a proper answer. If I own a factory, I will consider among my costs the prices that I have to pay for my inputs and the opportunity cost of tying up my money; and I will consider among the benefits the prices I receive for the finished product. But though the smoke from my chimneys imposes costs on my neighbors (inconvenience and health hazard), I do not bear those costs, and unless the law or my moral principles intervene, I do not consider them in making my plans. Thus I will produce more than is socially optimal (total social costs will be greater than total social benefits) because one of the real costs of production does not appear in *my* cost-benefit analysis.[21]

Here again we must ask whether certain externalities cause economic injustice. If every human being has a right (not a legal right but a moral right) to reasonably clean air, then the market that causes pollution is causing a distributive injustice.

When Nash addresses the externality problem, his first insight is that "short of terminating the entire human race, there is no way to end pollution. Even then, non-human life would continue the process of pollution to some extent." (p. 178)[22] Beyond this, Nash's response is typically free-market: if the government has to become involved in pollution control (or deal with other externalities), let it rely as much as possible on the market (e.g., by selling the rights to an optimal level of pollution). Weighing alternative ways to handle pollution is beyond the scope of this article. Rather let me make this important point: having admitted the *principle* of legitimate state involvement with public goods and externalities, Nash misleads by burying it in antistate rhetoric. Policy implications of such a principle ought to be given an important place in the Christian social-philosopher's thinking and writing.

7. Finally, the market will not provide, in a just manner, what I call "fundamental goods," so called because each individual has a

---

21. Note that even social cost-benefit analysis raises problems of economic justice. For expediency (social benefits greater than social costs) does not ensure that the people who bear the costs are the ones who should do so.

22. Now we know what Ronald Reagan was reading when he made his comment about the trees!

fundamental right to these goods regardless of her level of wealth or income.[23] Fundamental goods are things like education and health care, which, the Christian view of property and economic rights suggests, should be made available to all persons according to the extent of society's ability, without regard to the individual's own wealth or income. There are very difficult and profound questions involved here, of course. For example, if society cannot afford kidney machines for everyone with kidney illness, how should access to the machines be allocated? What seems to violate the Christian view of things, the Christian doctrine that God cares equally for all, is to say that the health care should go to those who can afford it—to auction off access to the kidney machines to the highest bidders.

Similar considerations apply to allocating educational opportunities. Education is so fundamental to a person's well-being, self-realization, and economic status that the conservative position seems to violate the Christian sense of justice. For the conservative, education is purely a private or family matter (although he may grudgingly admit certain positive externalities to having a minimally literate work force and citizenry), so in Nash's words, the state confuses moral with economic merit (pp. 58–59) if it tries to determine the distribution of educational benefits. But the education of the young is the responsibility of the entire community, since surely education is part of the "birthright" we spoke of earlier. And this birthright cannot be assured unless the state sees that the necessary resources are provided, regardless of "free-market" conditions.

What does a proper understanding of economic justice from a Christian (biblical) perspective imply about the role of the state? Nash holds that economic justice must be seen in terms of historically determined entitlements and that such a view leaves little room for state involvement in production, distribution, and redistribution. But as we have seen, the Bible teaches a high view of economic justice, which the laissez-faire market economy will not measure up to. Certainly justice in rectification requires a much more significant role than Nash envisions. And even if we completed rectification, setting everything "right" at a given time, the market would not by itself preserve economic justice. I

23. The concept of "fundamental goods" is close to that of "merit goods." See Richard Abel Musgrave, *The Theory of Public Finance: A Study in Public Economy* (1959); and John G. Head, *Public Goods and Public Welfare* (1974).

have not attempted a rigorous statement of the principles of justice in original acquisition, justice in transfer, or justice in rectification. Rather I have applied the biblical perspective in a more intuitive way. The larger task of working out the Christian principles of economic justice within the entitlement framework remains.

While much of Nash's argument is on the level of principle, there is also a constant strain of "practical" criticism—that the programs of the liberals just have not worked. Welfare programs destroy work incentives and price controls create shortages. While it is true that programs have been less than perfect, I suspect that if Nash looked with less jaundiced eyes, he would find more benefits than he expected.

But the shortcomings of our programs are not due primarily to ignorance of economics, as Nash repeatedly claims. Every microeconomics student can demonstrate how, given standard assumptions, rent controls create housing shortages and welfare programs can remove incentives to work, creating dependency. But Nash must remember that policies are created not by neutral philosopher-kings but by the give-and-take of a democratic process in which opinions and values often conflict and in which the chief concern of elected officials is to look out for the interests of the middle classes in their constituency. This public policy is often the result of compromises and, because it is piecemeal, it may not fit well with other policy. Despite these difficulties, the Christian should continue to support political programs that try to increase economic justice.

Study Questions

1. How does Beversluis define *economic justice*? How does his definition differ from Nash's?
2. How does Beversluis challenge Nash's distinction between universal and particular justice?
3. How does Beversluis differ with Nash's distinction between the biblical concepts of justice and love?
4. What kinds of responsibilities does Beversluis think Scripture requires of the state?
5. What is "justice in rectification," and why is this important to Beversluis's argument?
6. According to Beversluis, why does the market tend to create economic injustices?

A Reply to Eric Beversluis

Ronald H. Nash

On the very day that the first copy of *Freedom, Justice and the State* arrived from the publisher, I happened to take my family out to eat at a local Chinese restaurant. After the meal, as was our custom, we all took turns opening our fortune cookies and reading the message aloud. I was last. Breaking open the cookie, I carefully removed the little strip of white paper and found myself staring at the following message: "There is nothing so absurd that has not at some time been said by some philosopher." Receiving that exact message under those circumstances might have unsettled a less stalwart soul. For just an instant I considered the possibility that one of my former students like Richard Mouw or Donald Dayton might be in the restaurant's kitchen "fixing" the fortune cookies. As it turns out, both had alibis. Now I may have to ask Eric Beversluis where he was that evening. As we all know, however, prophecies by the oracle at Delphi, predictions by astrologers, and pronouncements in fortune cookies all partake of a convenient ambiguity. With that bit of encouragement, I undertake this response to Professor Beversluis.

The reader may feel that I spend about the first half of my response ignoring the substantive arguments Beversluis has directed against my position. In fact I start my response by trying to locate the really substantive disagreements between us. Then I point out important qualifications or clarifications of my position, overlooked by Beversluis, that effectively blunt many of his thrusts. And finally, as space permits, I shall deal decisively with his more important arguments.

Substantive Disagreements

It is important that the reader get a clear grasp of what Beversluis and I are arguing about. For one thing we are not really disagreeing over the proper *ends* of Christian social action. Neither of us believes that an affluent society like ours[1] should allow the truly needy, those who are completely incapable of helping themselves, to go without assistance. To the extent that providing aid for the truly needy in our society is a necessary objective of Christian social action, we agree.[2] For the most part the debate between conservatives and liberals on issues raised in Beversluis's article is a dispute over *means* and not ends.

Beversluis and I also agree that this assistance to the truly needy requires some role for the state.[3] My book is clear in stating that neither the mechanism of the market nor private charity will solve the problem. Perhaps because my book contains so many negative comments about government, Beversluis failed to give proper place to my admission that the state still has an indispensable role in relieving social misery. An important part of my position is that too often such attempts by the state have only increased the misery.

Where do Beversluis and I differ? We certainly disagree over the proper grade that should be given to liberal social programs. Beversluis thinks they deserve an *A* for effort and perhaps a *B* for results. I give them a high *F*. While Beversluis admits at the end of

1. At least our society was still somewhat affluent at the time of writing.

2. One secondary goal of *Freedom, Justice and the State* (1980) was to show that this conviction is shared by conservative social theorists who may not share the Christian values of Beversluis and myself. No one wants to see poor people starving, freezing to death, or dying without proper medical care. To suggest that conservatives do not care is arrogant slander. The proper question is, What is the most effective way for society to meet the needs of the truly needy?

3. Another goal of *Freedom, Justice and the State* was to show that all conservative social theorists agree on this point. Radical libertarians do not agree; but they are not conservatives and I am not a libertarian. So their disclaimer is irrelevant so far as my position is concerned.

his paper that liberal social programs since Franklin Roosevelt and especially since Lyndon Johnson have not been unqualified successes, he still concludes that they have done more good than bad and deserve the continued support of Christians. This coded message translates into: "Keep voting for liberal Democrats and Republicans." Since 1965 or the beginning of the programs of the Great Society, spending for social welfare at all levels of government has increased more than fivefold. But in spite of this massive increase, the number of poor people in the United States has remained constant, a fact that raises questions about the effectiveness of the liberal approach. Walter E. Williams, a prominent black economist, pointed out in 1979 that the cumulative total spent at every level of American government just to fight poverty was $250 billion a year.[4] Had this amount of money been distributed equally to all families below the poverty level, each of them would have received an annual payment of $34,000. The obvious reason why this amount never reaches the poor is the massive bureaucratic system that has grown up with the welfare state, which siphons off most of the money before it reaches the poor and which, my book suggests, is the real beneficiary of liberal social programs. Another black economist, Thomas Sowell, states: "The amount necessary to lift every man, woman, and child in America above the poverty line has been calculated, and it is *one-third* of what is in fact spent on poverty programs. Clearly, much of the transfer ends up in the pockets of highly paid administrators, consultants, and staff as well as higher-income recipients of benefits from programs advertised as anti-poverty efforts."[5] Surely the bucket used to carry money from the pockets of the taxpayer to the poor is leaking badly. *Freedom, Justice and the State* suggests that the real beneficiaries of liberal social programs are not the poor and disadvantaged but the members of the governmental bureaucracy that administers the programs. I do not wish to impugn the motives of all who call themselves liberals. But neither should one overlook the fact that the army of bureaucrats whose business is "helping the poor" are doing considerably better than those they are supposed to be helping.

4. Obviously the passage of time has made the 1979 figure seem like a pittance. See also Thomas Sowell, *Race and Economics* (1975), pp. 195–200.

5. "The Uses of Government for Racial Equality," *National Review*, 4 September 1981, p. 1013.

Beversluis and I also disagree over the identification of the truly needy. Obviously our country contains many unfortunate children and adults who face insurmountable medical bills, who are unable to work or who cannot find work, who cannot help themselves. But does Beversluis wish to deny that large numbers of people in this country benefit from economic redistribution who can be regarded as needy only in a grossly extended sense of the word? Do middle-class college students really have a *right* to subsidized loans or food stamps? Moreover, liberal social programs have often been so shortsighted and so poorly designed that they have resulted in large numbers of people being forced into a slavish dependence on the state. Liberal social programs can be compared to heroin addiction. Once dependence is established, the continual supply of what was supposed to be a temporary palliation becomes a matter of life and death. People come to view the temporary dole as their never-ending right.

Beversluis and I also disagree over the size and power of the bureaucracy needed to aid the truly needy. Conservatives have, for years, urged an end to the myriad programs presently in existence in favor of the adoption of one simple and far more cost-effective means of transferring money from one group to another. This means is a negative income tax, which should not be confused with the parody discussed during Richard Nixon's presidency. Once in place, the negative income tax would eliminate the need for the massive welfare bureaucracy presently in place; it would transfer funds directly to the poor; and it would give real incentives for those able to work to terminate their slavish dependence on the state.

Many advocates of the welfare state paint a picture of an unending flow of cash from the producers in society to the non-producers. The liberal's obsession with the proper distribution of society's goods blinds him to the vital truth that before society can have enough to distribute among its needy, a sufficient quantity of wealth must first be *produced*. To the extent that social programs to help the poor discourage the production of wealth, they are self-defeating.

Much more needs to be said about all this. But of course much of it has already been stated in *Freedom, Justice and the State* and the scores of books and articles cited there.

Beversluis's Oversights

My comments to this point have sought to clarify some of the more important ways in which Beversluis and I agree and disagree. I now turn my attention to several important views found in *Freedom, Justice and the State* that Beversluis ignores. My comments here are important because my position cannot be understood or appreciated without these clarifications and qualifications. A number of Beversluis's objections are directed against a straw man.

First of all, Beversluis completely misses the central point of my book and thus misstates my basic thesis. According to him, "Nash's thesis is that *social* justice does not require statist involvement" (p. 27 above). A fundamental premise of my position is the distinction between the state and statism; consequently there is a crucial difference in my view between *state involvement* and *statist involvement*. My book makes it clear that my opposition is not so much to the institution of the state per se as it is to statism, a difference as great as that between sex and fornication. Statism, among other things, is the dangerous expansion of governmental power and influence over the individual and voluntary societies that, in its final stages, ends in totalitarianism. My book suggests that many degrees of statism are possible. I am certain, for example, that Beversluis is a more moderate statist than Fidel Castro. While I call my own position "anti-statism," it is a much more moderate form of anti-statism than one finds represented in the writings of, for example, many contemporary libertarians, some of whom are anarchists. Beversluis's description of my position as holding "that social justice does not require statist involvement" is misleading because his reader will conclude that my view precludes *state involvement*, which is a horse of another color.

To eliminate any possible confusion, let me spell out my thesis with respect to justice. First, the claim that social justice requires the necessary support and active intervention of a large, powerful, and paternalistic state is an essential part of the liberal political creed. The liberal establishment in America frequently justifies the forcible imposition of new social policy on the ground that it is mandated by the demands of social justice. Only an increase in the size and power of the state, only a greater concentration of power in the central government, the liberal believes, can provide a framework within which justice can thrive. The basic thesis of my book is that this liberal thesis is unjustified. I go on to maintain that what are often thought to constitute arguments for the liberal thesis reflect a number of fundamental errors, some of which are noted in the passage Beversluis quotes at the beginning of his article.

Beversluis is also inattentive to important features of my exposition and defense of free-market economics. My approach to economics is grounded on the work of the Austrian school of economics, a movement that some careless economists fail to distinguish adequately from the Chicago school of Milton Friedman. Key elements of the Austrian approach successfully blunt many of the most frequently cited objections to capitalism, arguments that predictably appear in Beversluis's paper. For example, Beversluis raises the old argument that free-market economics depends upon the possibility of perfect competition and perfect knowledge, neither of which is attainable in the real world. Had he been more familiar with the Austrian position, he would have known better than to mention issues made irrelevant by the Austrian revolution in economics.[6]

My defense of capitalism is predicated on much more than the customary claims one hears about the importance of private property and individual liberty and the fact that the system works better than any alternative. I argue that free-market exchange benefits society by transmitting information about the needs and desires of countless numbers of individuals. As entrepreneurs (risk-takers) attend to this information, the needs of society are met in a truly amazing way. Governmental intervention in the market effectively destroys the informational function of the market. Because the central planners in an interventionist economy lack this vital information, centralized economic planning produces chaos: the wrong goods in the wrong amounts are produced and shipped to the wrong places. Empirical support for

---

6. My book pointed this out, of course, but Beversluis must have rushed through these pages. The best sources for Austrian economics are the writings of Ludwig von Mises and Friedrich August von Hayek. Some of the most exciting work in Austrian economics is currently being done by Israel M. Kirzner. The most important works are cited in *Freedom, Justice and the State*. A popular introduction to the subject is Henry Hazlitt, "Understanding 'Austrian' Economics," *The Freeman* 31 (February 1981): 67–78. In this same connection I must object to Beversluis's repeated references to my position as "laissez-faire," a term I reject. Beversluis's practice is an example of a persuasive definition.

this claim may be gathered by anyone willing to submit himself to life in a Soviet satellite.

Society also benefits from the risks that entrepreneurs take; often they pioneer in offering new or improved goods and services. Socialism discourages risk-taking by confiscating the rewards of the risk-takers who are fortunate enough to succeed and sharing their winnings with those who refused to take any risks. This kind of economic redistribution cuts a vital nerve of economic activity that benefits society and its poor in countless ways.

Arthur Shenfield, a prominent British economist and barrister, has recently pointed out another fact about capitalism that I tried to stress in *Freedom, Justice and the State:*

> Men have always wanted to be rich, whatever the precepts of their religions may have been. Until the rise of capitalism the most effective way to become rich was to seize men's bodies or land. . . . Capitalism was the first system in human history to harness the desire to become rich to the peaceful supply of men's abundance.

Shenfield goes on to consider one ground of resentment against such a system of exchange:

> . . . since envy abides powerfully among most of us, the desire of other men to be rich remains a prominent object of our censure; and since capitalism is the most effective agent for making all men rich, especially the erstwhile poor, its very success makes it the target for hostility, particularly from intellectuals who can see nothing in it but getting and spending. But men still want to get rich. The alternative to serving other men's wants is seizing power over them, as it always has been. Hence it is not surprising that wherever the enemies of capitalism have prevailed, the result has been not only the debasement of consumption standards for the masses but also their reduction to serfdom by the new privileged class of socialist rulers.[7]

Obviously all kinds of predictable objections will come to the minds of those who have been taught to associate the word *cap-*

---

7. "Capitalism Under the Tests of Ethics," *Imprimis* 10 (December 1981): 4–5. (*Imprimis* is the monthly journal of Hillsdale College, Hillsdale, Mich.)

italism with everything that is wrong in the world. Since most of those objections are covered in the last two chapters of *Freedom, Justice and the State*, I shall drop this subject and turn directly to Beversluis's article.

Economic and Distributive Justice

Beversluis begins his argument by begging the most basic question in the entire debate. He simply assumes that a just economic system is one that redistributes people's holdings to fit a preconceived pattern. The reader should not be confused by such phrases as "legitimate claims" and "fair share" in Beversluis's definition of a just economic system. Later in his paper he gives those vague phrases a content that makes the unstated egalitarianism of his definition explicit.

Beversluis's treatment of economic justice and distributive justice as synonyms is also a neat move that helps to stack the deck for some of his later arguments. The only problem is that it too begs the question. The notions of economic and distributive justice clearly are not equivalent. While there are times when distributive justice is concerned with the distribution of *economic* goods (like welfare payments and food stamps), it is often the case that the scope of distributive justice is noneconomic. For example, the criteria used to determine who will be subject to a military draft or the distribution of grades in a philosophy course are questions of distributive justice. But these latter kinds of distributive justice obviously are not instances of economic justice.

The Notion of Justice

One of the more important claims of *Freedom, Justice and the State* is that evangelical social liberals are inattentive to important distinctions within the notion of justice. This confusion compromises much of their appeal to biblical uses of "justice" since they simply assume that biblical endorsements of justice are in fact divine commands to support economic redistribution. Beversluis thinks he discovers a fatal flaw in my analysis by suggesting that particular justice is really only a species of universal justice. Before we can see who is right, it is necessary to put my argument in context. Using Aristotle's discussion of justice as my

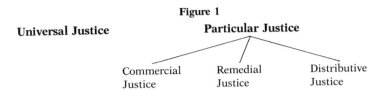

starting point, I distinguished among the types of justice included in figure 1.

We seldom use the word *justice* in Aristotle's universal sense any more. But this usage was very common in the ancient world. Plato talked about this kind of justice, and it is prominent throughout the Bible. Universal justice is synonymous with personal righteousness. We might call it *justice as virtue*. So when the Bible says that Noah was a just man, it does not mean that he voted the straight Democratic ticket or sent money to Salvadoran guerrillas. It simply means that he was virtuous.[8] *Particular justice* is especially concerned with fairness. The man or woman who is just in the particular sense does not seek more than his fair share; we could characterize particular justice as *justice as fairness*. Fairness comes into play in many areas of life. Identifying three contexts where this kind of justice is especially important, Aristotle referred to commercial, remedial, and distributive justice. Commercial justice is the kind of justice one looks for in economic transactions; if a seller shortchanges or overcharges a customer, his action is unfair or unjust in the commercial sense. Remedial or corrective justice is the justice that should prevail in a court of law. Distributive justice is present or absent in situations where some good or burden is to be distributed between two or more people.

Two questions must now be asked:

1. What is the relationship between particular justice on the one hand and, on the other, commercial, remedial, and distributive justice? The answer is obvious. All three are species of particular justice. Particular justice means treating people fairly; commercial, remedial, and distributive justice are supposed to characterize the different kinds of settings in which the question of fair treatment arises.

2. But what is the relationship between universal and par-

---

8. See *Freedom, Justice and the State*, chap. 2, for an amplification of this point and others that follow.

ticular justice? Here is where Beversluis makes one of the more serious errors in his paper. He simply assumes that particular justice is a species of universal justice. This leads him to write: "Clearly the particular virtue of justice . . . is *part of* universal justice. . . . But then if the Bible mandates universal justice, it thereby mandates its parts, including distributive (economic) justice." (p. 28 above) Perhaps Beversluis got confused by Aristotle's labels. I suppose it would be easy to conclude that Aristotle used "particular" because he viewed this other type of justice as a part of universal justice. But that view is wrong. Universal justice is universal because it is a kind of justice that can be practiced by all human beings; it is not necessary for a person to occupy a particular role or be in a particular situation in order to be personally righteous. One can be just in the universal sense whether or not he is a businessman or a judge or someone charged with the responsibility of distributing some good. Universal justice is universal because we normally hope to find this justice present in every human being; it is supposed to be universal in scope. Being virtuous should not depend upon one's being in a particular type of situation. But particular justice is situational in the sense that people can practice these kinds of justice if and only if they are in a particular type of situation. A person can practice commercial justice if and only if he is involved in an economic exchange. A person can practice remedial justice if and only if he occupies one of several possible roles with regard to criminal or civil law. And a person can practice distributive justice if and only if his situation involves him in the distribution of some good or some burden. The reason why commercial, remedial, and distributive justice are types of particular justice, then, is because they are possible only for people who find themselves in particular situations. Beversluis's claim that particular justice is a species of universal justice, then, is mistaken. Consequently the trump card he plays in his argument turns out to be a joker.

It may help if I go on to point out, with regard to the forms of particular justice, that a distinction can be drawn between *practicing justice* and *promoting justice*. The various kinds of particular justice can be *practiced* only by people who occupy certain positions or fill certain roles. But all of us can do things that will *promote* the various kinds of particular justice; for example, we can promote remedial justice by working for the election of honest and competent judges.

The argument of *Freedom, Justice and the State* stands. When one reads the writings of evangelical social liberals and liberation theologians carefully, he will find many distressingly bad examples of biblical exegesis. While the full context of their alleged proof-texts makes it clear that the Bible is talking about personal righteousness, they take undue liberties with the text and simply assume that numerous biblical allusions to justice are endorsements of economic redistribution.

Since a detailed analysis of Beversluis's remarks about love and justice would require far more space than I have at my disposal, I must content myself with a very brief summary of where his argument goes astray. (1) I find serious confusions of my position in his exposition. At one point, for example, he takes a statement that functions as a premise in my argument, calls it a conclusion, and then faults me because my "conclusion" does not follow. (2) His argument appears to contain several examples of the fallacy of equivocation (hint: check out his usage of words like *discriminate* and *impersonal*). (3) For all the thunder and lightning in these paragraphs, his conclusion is the modest claim that love and justice may sometimes be closely related, a point with which I am happy to agree. But I have trouble seeing how this conclusion should cause me to reconsider my claim that evangelical social activists often write as though love and justice are equivalent.

Biblical Texts

Beversluis accuses me of being curiously selective in the biblical texts about justice that I consider in *Freedom, Justice and the State*. The charge is surprising since the texts I cite are precisely those quoted in the writings of evangelical liberals and liberation theologians.[9] I should think that Beversluis would have known this. I find the "new" texts that he cites even more curious. Beversluis's handling of his texts is an excellent example of one recurring error in most such appeals to the Bible, the failure to

---

9. I refer to some of these works in *Freedom, Justice and the State*. One book that has appeared since then and that appeals to the same texts I consider is Stephen Charles Mott, *Biblical Ethics and Social Change* (1982). For another example see Robert K. Johnston, *Evangelicals at an Impasse: Biblical Authority in Practice* (1979).

distinguish between the *interpretation* of a text and its *application*. I find very little attention given to interpretation in Beversluis's article. Anxious to make his point, he simply quotes the passage in question and jumps immediately to what he regards as the self-evident application, completely skipping in the process important questions about the interpretation of the text. As an example, consider his use of Exodus 22:26–27. The verses state that if a neighbor has turned over his cloak as collateral for a loan and if that neighbor has no other way to protect himself from the cold, then the person holding the cloak should make it available during times when it is needed. Interpreting the passage poses no special problems. But on the basis of the text, Beversluis then writes: "A person has a right to the material goods she or he needs for a decent existence. Thus the Bible teaches that there are rights to specific kinds of economic goods, and that these rights bind governments as well as individuals." (p. 32 above) Wow! He gets all this from those two simple verses? Not really, of course, since once again he is taking all sorts of things for granted and reading his conclusions into the text. In other words he is practicing eisegesis, not exegesis.

Suppose we see how I would apply the text (as opposed to interpret it) to myself. The only obvious application I see is this: if I lend an individual money and he assigns as collateral for that loan something that he subsequently needs in order to meet some temporary emergency, then I have an obligation not to withhold that which he needs for that time. But what does Beversluis extract from the text? Before one knows it, he has used it to find a theory of state-enforced economic redistribution in the Bible: "Thus the Bible teaches that there are rights to specific kinds of economic goods, and that these rights bind governments as well as individuals."[10] Now it may be true that people have economic rights that bind governments. But I submit that one cannot find this doctrine in Exodus 22.

As I have stated, one important hermeneutical principle commonly ignored by evangelical social activists is the distinction between interpretation and application. Another principle that they shortchange in their treatment of Scripture is the importance of reading a passage in the light of its context. Beversluis

10. I will return to Beversluis's point about economic rights shortly.

says nothing about the other verses in Exodus 22; I do not blame him. How many of the injunctions contained in Exodus 22 does he want his government to sanction? If the rest of the chapter is treated in the same way as he handles verses 26–27, Beversluis's state is negligent in a number of other ways. Exodus 22:18–20 are sufficient to make my point. If Exodus 22 contains a list of duties for any just state, then one must conclude that the contemporary state has a duty to execute witches, sex perverts, and idolaters. As Jacob J. Petuchowski of Hebrew Union College points out: "It becomes a matter of biblical exegesis and hermeneutics to determine whether or not the biblical texts, originally addressed to a primitive agrarian society, really commit the latter-day believer to an espousal of socialism in the modern world. . . . Still, it is quite possible to produce one-sided and partisan collections of biblical and rabbinic proof-texts which would clearly demonstrate that religion commits us to this or that political program or social action platform."[11]

From their own proof-texts Beversluis and George N. Monsma deduce a set of principles. Most of them deserve consideration, regardless of how questionable their derivation from Scripture may be. But one near the end of the list gives the game away: "Place limits on the concentration of wealth, income, and economic power in the society. . . ." (p. 33 above). Beversluis admits that this principle is not derived from Scripture so much as it is a necessary condition for the realization of his platform. Again Beversluis simply begs the question, in this case assuming that other and less drastic means are not available that will make possible the realization of his other ends. As I read Monsma's principle, he is calling for the state to exercise control over individual income and wealth to a far greater degree than it has yet done in the United States.

One of the more surprising aspects of all the current interest in finding biblical passages that can support a collectivist economic ideology is this: while people exhibit great ingenuity in discovering hitherto unrecognized implications in ambiguous Old Testament passages, hardly anyone bothers to look at several clear texts in the New Testament. Consider just one:

11. "The Altar/Throne Clash Updated," *Christianity Today*, 23 September 1977, p. 20.

> In the name of the Lord Jesus Christ, we command you, brothers, to keep away from every brother who is idle and does not live according to the teaching you received from us. For you yourselves know how you ought to follow our example. We were not idle when we were with you, nor did we eat anyone's food without paying for it. On the contrary, we worked night and day, laboring and toiling so that we would not be a burden to any of you. . . . For even when we were with you, we gave you this rule: "If a man will not work, he shall not eat." We hear that some among you are idle. They are not busy; they are busybodies. Such people we command and urge in the Lord Jesus Christ, to settle down and earn the bread they eat.[12]

Without wishing to sound irreverent, I must add that these words were written not by Ronald Reagan but by the apostle Paul.

The way Beversluis handles the doctrine of Christian stewardship ought to cause a few eyes to blink. No believer should deny that God is the ultimate owner of all that we possess; we are simply stewards or trustees of what he has blessed us with. But if I read Beversluis correctly, he twists the doctrine of man's stewardship under God into the view that the believer must surrender his will and judgment concerning his holdings to God's surrogate on earth, the state. I suppose it is thinking along this same line that leads some liberation theologians to view Marxist terrorists as God's proxies.[13]

Almost all of Beversluis's argument stands or falls on the claim that the poor have economic rights that bind individuals and states to actions that will recognize those rights. If we overlook the fact that Beversluis's attempt to infer this position from Scripture fails (leaving his position unsupported, for the time being), his claim is interesting and worthy of more detailed study in another context. I have even toyed with the idea myself. The problem for now is that Beversluis's discussion is too incomplete to permit any final decision about his theory. For one thing, Beversluis does not show that these economic rights are in fact what we call "demand rights," which they would have to be in order to function in his argument.[14] Even if Beversluis some day fills in

12. 2 Thess. 3:6–8, 10–12; see also 1 Thess. 4:11–12 and Eph. 4:28.
13. Obviously this last sentence does not apply to Beversluis or Monsma.
14. The United Nations Declaration of Human Rights contains several examples of human rights that are clearly not demand rights. For example, the decla-

the gaps and succeeds in showing that the economic rights of the poor are demand rights that entail corresponding obligations, he would then have to show that his cryptosocialist means are the only or the best means to secure those rights.

Original Acquisition and Rectification

Finally, Beversluis writes: "Nash makes serious errors in his use of Nozickean analysis. . . ." (p. 36 above). While Beversluis makes the whole matter sound very serious, what do these alleged errors amount to? His argument revolves around the following three propositions:

1. Nash's book does not discuss justice in original acquisition or justice in rectification.

2. Nash himself has no theory of justice in original acquisition and no theory of justice in rectification.

3. Nash does not believe that justice includes the notion of rectification.

Not only does Beversluis think that all three of these propositions are true, he believes that both 2 and 3 follow from 1. As any freshman logic student knows, the inferences from 1 to 2 or from 1 to 3 are invalid. Neither 2 nor 3 follows from 1; the mystery is that Beversluis thinks they do. Since my book discusses neither justice in original acquisition nor justice in rectification, the question becomes, how does Beversluis *know* that 2 and 3 are true? The obvious answer is that he does not know. If there really is any question about my beliefs on the subject, I am quite happy to declare for the record that both 2 and 3 are false. Beversluis confuses silence on an issue with opposition to it. Certainly I believe that justice will take account of people's entitlements. But entitlements do not exist in a vacuum. Justice with regard to entitlements will depend on how people's holdings were acquired and will take account of the possible need for rectification. The careful reader will recall that Beversluis does not give us any details of *his* theory of justice in original acquisition or justice in rectification. But it is not difficult to imagine, given the direction

---

ration states that all human beings have a right to marry. If this were a demand right and if some especially obnoxious person had this right, then some other unfortunate person would have the duty of marrying him.

of his remarks, the broad outline of his theories. It should be just as easy to see where my own analysis of original acquisition and rectification would differ from his.[15]

The Austrian School

The arguments hinted at in the last third of Beversluis's paper are disappointing for two related reasons. First, some of them are irrelevant because they fail to take account of how economists of the Austrian school approach these problems. Instead of raising the outdated claims that a free-market economy can be faulted because it presumes perfect knowledge and perfect competition, he should have examined the Austrian analysis that neither perfect knowledge nor perfect competition is required in a market economy. But this leads into my second point. One of the more troubling things about Beversluis's paper is his apparent lack of awareness of the revolution in economic thought that has been taking place during the last ten years, a revolution grounded in the writings of Ludwig von Mises and Friedrich August von Hayek and articulated by such thinkers as Israel M. Kirzner, Walter E. Williams, and Thomas Sowell.[16] Conservative economists are producing an impressive body of literature. It is unfortunate that the arguments Beversluis offers in support of increasing the economic and political power of the state overlook that literature.

Study Questions

1. Is Aristotle's distinction between universal and particular senses of justice helpful? What useful insights did you receive from the debate between Nash and Beversluis concerning this distinction?
2. Are there important distinctions in principle between Nash and Beversluis concerning the state's rightful role in estab-

15. For a further discussion of my views regarding justice in original acquisition and in rectification, see my *Social Justice and the Christian Church*, chap. 4.

16. As just one example of an analysis of a contemporary problem from the perspective of Austrian economics, consider Thomas Sowell, *Markets and Minorities* (1981). Also worth consulting is Louis M. Spadaro, ed., *New Directions in Austrian Economics* (1978).

lishing and maintaining economic justice, or are the differences more a matter of degree?

3. What relevance do Old Testament regulations (for example, those in Exodus 22) have to the way we understand the nature of economic justice?

4. How would you distinguish between the biblical concepts of love and justice? What do these distinctions imply about government's function in society?

5. To what extent are Nash's and Beversluis's differences affected by their divergent views of recent social-welfare programs?

Biblical Resources for Further Study 4

The Character of Biblical Justice

Examine the following biblical texts determined to enlarge your understanding of the word *justice*. Using a theological wordbook, Bible dictionary, or Bible concordance, pursue other texts that shed additional light on this dimension of God's character.

1. Justice: an attribute of God

   Deuteronomy 32:4
   Deuteronomy 10:17–21
   Psalm 35:10
   Psalm 146:5–9

   Questions
   a. What characteristics of God are described in these passages?
   b. How does the Old Testament practically explain God's character when it describes him as a God of justice?

2. God's judgment on the unjust

   Amos 8:4–8
   Micah 3:1–4
   Zechariah 7:9–12

Questions

    c. What is God's attitude toward injustice and violence?
    d. What happens to a society in which injustice reigns?

3. Who are the "truly needy"?

Deuteronomy 14:28–29
Jeremiah 22:1–5
Matthew 25:31–46

Questions

    e. In the Old Testament passages, what categories of people are singled out for special care and what did each group have in common?
    f. What did Jesus teach about the same groups of people?

4. "Being holy" and "doing justice"

Micah 6:6–8
Isaiah 58

Questions

    g. How does the prophet Micah summarize what God requires of us?
    h. According to Isaiah, what kind of worship does God desire? How does the prophet link holy living with doing justice?

Summary Questions

1. Do these passages shed any light on the debate between Nash and Beversluis concerning a universal and particular sense of justice?
2. What insights do these passages give us about the identity of the "truly needy" and how they should be cared for?

Government's Obligation to Administer Justice

Carefully study the following passages of Scripture to deepen your understanding of the government's role in God's created order. With the aid of Bible commentaries and handbooks, study the context of these passages as well.

1. The creation of civil authority in Israel

   Exodus 18:13–27
   Leviticus 19:13–18

   Questions

   a. What kind of government structure did Moses create for the twelve tribes of Israel?
   b. What are some basic instructions in Leviticus 19:13–18 concerning the way society should function?

2. King David's view of political leadership that is just

   2 Samuel 23:1–4
   1 Chronicles 18:14

   Questions

   c. What was King David's description of a ruler who governs righteously?
   d. How does Scripture summarize David's reign?

3. The impact of political leadership that is just

   Proverbs 16:12
   Proverbs 29:4
   Proverbs 29:14
   Isaiah 10:1–3

   Questions

   e. What are the consequences of just political leadership?
   f. What is the link between just political rule and political stability?

4. The New Testament view of government

   Romans 13:1–7
   1 Peter 2:13–17

   Questions

   g. What are the principal functions of a government?
   h. Do these functions differ from those described in the Old Testament? If so, how?

Summary Questions

1. What conclusions can we draw from these passages concerning the proper role of government in society?
2. What insights can we gain from these materials about the limits of governmental authority?

Economic Justice

The following passages are a small percentage of those referring to just economic activity. For other passages and for discussion of the economic, political, and social context of Hebrew society, see books in the bibliography.

1. Biblical stewardship

   Genesis 1–3
   Genesis 9:1–7

   Questions

   a. What responsibility did God give to human beings before the fall? How did he alter this after the fall?
   b. What were God's instructions to Noah and his family after the flood?

2. God's ownership and maintenance of creation

   Colossians 1:16–20
   Hebrews 1:1–4
   Matthew 6:25–30

   Questions

   c. What is Jesus Christ's relationship to creation at present?
   d. What are some practical economic implications of believing that God owns and sustains the universe? How does Matthew 6 instruct us to live in light of this reality?

3. Old Testament regulations concerning a just economy

   Leviticus 19:9–10
   Leviticus 25:1–55

   Questions

   e. What underlying concerns are expressed in these instructions concerning harvesting and the year of Jubilee?

   f. What insights do these regulations give us into the structure or limits of economic activity?

4. New Testament insights on economic justice

   Acts 2:42–47
   Acts 4:32–35
   Ephesians 4:28
   2 Thessalonians 3:6–10

   Questions

   g. What do Acts 2 and 4 teach us about the early church's economic behavior?

   h. What did Paul say about those who are able but who refuse to work?

Summary Questions

1. How does a proper understanding of our stewardship affect the way we comprehend the nature of economic justice?
2. What should be our primary concerns as we work together to create just economic structures and as we engage individually in economic activity?

The Biblical Norms of Love and Justice

The following passages focus on the biblical concept of love and should be compared to the four passages given above in the section "The Character of Biblical Justice."

1. The "love commandment" of Jesus Christ

   Matthew 5:43–48
   Matthew 22:34–40

   Questions

   a. How would you summarize the central teachings of Jesus?

   b. What did Jesus add to Old Testament teaching on the subject of love?

2. The practical implementation of love

Luke 10:25–37
Matthew 25:31–46

Questions

c. What does the parable of the good Samaritan teach us about the nature of God's love?
d. What does the picture of the final judgment in Matthew 25 say about how we can demonstrate our love for Jesus?

3. Early church teachings about love

1 Corinthians 13
1 John 3:11–24

Questions

e. How do these qualities of love compare with the characteristics of justice discussed earlier?
f. What are the primary aspects of the love described in these passages?

Summary Questions

1. Can institutions that utilize force be instruments of God's love?
2. If love and justice are both dimensions of God's character and thus are not incompatible, what differentiates them from each other?

Selected Bibliography

Books Cited

Arthur, John, and Shaw, William H., eds. *Justice and Economic Distribution*. Englewood Cliffs, N.J.: Prentice-Hall, 1978.

Boadway, Robin W. *Public Sector Economics*. Cambridge, Mass.: Winthrop, 1979.

Bowie, Norman E., and Simon, Robert L. *The Individual and the Political Order: An Introduction to Social and Political Philosophy*. Englewood Cliffs, N.J.: Prentice-Hall, 1977.

Burnham, James. *Suicide of the West: An Essay on the Meaning and Destiny of Liberalism*. New Rochelle: Arlington, 1964.

Cullmann, Oscar. *The State in the New Testament*. New York: Scribner, 1956.

Evans, M. Stanton. *Clear and Present Dangers: A Conservative View of America's Government*. Edited by James David Barber. New York: Harcourt Brace Jovanovich, 1975.

French, Peter A.; Uehling, Theodore E., Jr.; and Wettstein, Howard K.: eds. *Studies in Ethical Theory*. Midwest Studies in Philosophy, vol. 3. Morris: University of Minnesota, 1978.

Friedman, Milton, and Friedman, Rose D. *Capitalism and Freedom*. Chicago: University of Chicago, 1962.

Hayek, Friedrich August von. *The Constitution of Liberty*. Chicago: Regnery, 1972.

———. *Law, Legislation and Liberty: A New Statement of the Liberal Principles of Justice and Political Economy*. 3 vols. Chicago: University of Chicago, 1973–1979.

Head, John G. *Public Goods and Public Welfare*. Durham, N.C.: Duke University, 1974.

Heilbroner, Robert L. *The Making of Economic Society*. 6th ed. Englewood Cliffs, N.J.: Prentice-Hall, 1980.

Held, Virginia, ed. *Property, Profits, and Economic Justice*. Belmont, Calif.: Wadsworth, 1980.

Johnston, Robert K. *Evangelicals at an Impasse: Biblical Authority in Practice*. Atlanta: John Knox, 1979.

Meyer, Frank S. *In Defense of Freedom: A Conservative Credo*. Chicago: Regnery, 1962.

———, ed. *What Is Conservatism?* New York: Holt, Rinehart and Winston, 1964.

Mott, Stephen Charles. *Biblical Ethics and Social Change*. New York: Oxford University, 1982.

Musgrave, Richard Abel. *The Theory of Public Finance: A Study in Public Economy*. New York: McGraw-Hill, 1959.

Nash, George H. *The Conservative Intellectual Movement in America, Since 1945*. New York: Basic, 1976.

Nash, Ronald H. *Freedom, Justice and the State*. Lanham, Md.: University Press of America, 1980.

———. *Social Justice and the Christian Church*. Milford, Mich.: Mott Media, 1983.

Nicholson, Walter. *Microeconomic Theory: Basic Principles and Extensions*. 2d ed. Hinsdale, Ill.: Dryden, 1978.

Nozick, Robert. *Anarchy, State, and Utopia*. New York: Basic, 1974.

Polanyi, Karl. *The Great Transformation*. New York: Farrar & Rinehart, 1944.

Röpke, Wilhelm. *Economics of the Free Society*. Translated by Patrick M. Boarman. Chicago: Regnery, 1963.

———. *A Humane Economy: The Social Framework of the Free Market*. Translated by Elizabeth Henderson. Chicago: Regnery, 1960.

Sowell, Thomas. *Markets and Minorities*. New York: Basic, 1981.

———. *Race and Economics*. New York: McKay, 1975.

Spadaro, Louis M., ed. *New Directions in Austrian Economics.* Studies in Economic Theory. Kansas City, Kan.: Sheed Andrews and McMeel, 1978.

von Mises, Ludwig. *Human Action: A Treatise on Economics.* New Haven: Yale University, 1949.

Additional Resources

Beckmann, David M. *Where Faith and Economics Meet: A Christian Critique.* Minneapolis: Augsburg, 1981.

Birch, Bruce C., and Rasmussen, Larry L. *The Predicament of the Prosperous.* Philadelphia: Westminster, 1978.

Clouse, Robert G., ed. *Wealth and Poverty: Four Christian Views of Economics.* Downers Grove, Ill.: InterVarsity, 1984. Gary North writes on "Free Market Capitalism"; William E. Diehl, on "The Guided-Market System"; Art Gish, on "Decentralist Economics"; and John Gladwin, on "Centralist Economics."

Ellul, Jacques. *Money and Power.* Translated by LaVonne Neff. Downers Grove, Ill.: InterVarsity, 1984.

Goudzwaard, Bob. *Aid for the Overdeveloped West.* Toronto: Wedge, 1975.

_____. *Idols of Our Time.* Translated by Mark Vander Vennen. Downers Grove, Ill.: InterVarsity, 1984.

Griffiths, Brian. *The Creation of Wealth: A Christian's Case for Capitalism.* Downers Grove, Ill.: InterVarsity, 1984.

_____. *Morality and the Market Place.* Hodder & Stoughton, 1982.

Hay, Donald. *A Christian Critique of Capitalism.* Bramcote, Notts.: Grove, 1975.

Houck, John W., and Williams, Oliver F., eds. *Catholic Social Teaching and the United States Economy: Working Papers for a Bishops' Pastoral.* Washington, D.C.: University Press of America, 1984.

Nash, Ronald H., ed. *Liberation Theology.* Milford, Mich.: Mott Media, 1984.

Novak, Michael. *The Spirit of Democratic Capitalism.* New York: Simon and Schuster, 1982.

Schumacher, E. F. *Small Is Beautiful: Economics As If People Mattered.* New York: Harper & Row, 1973.

Sider, Ronald J., ed. *Cry Justice! The Bible on Hunger and Poverty.* Downers Grove, Ill.: InterVarsity, 1980.

Wright, Christopher J. H. *An Eye for an Eye: The Place of Old Testament Ethics Today.* Downers Grove, Ill.: InterVarsity, 1983.

Index of Scripture References

Genesis

chaps 1–3   **70**
6:9   **20, 28**
9:1–7   **70**

Exodus

18:13–27   **69**
chap 22   **60–61, 65**
22:18–20   **61**
22:26–27   **32, 60, 61**
23:3   **20**
23:3–6   **11**
23:6   **20**

Leviticus

19:9–10   **70**
19:13–18   **69**
19:36   **11, 21**
25:1–55   **70**

Deuteronomy

10:17–21   **67**
14:28–29   **68**
32:4   **67**

2 Samuel

23:1–4   **69**
23:3   **21, 28**

1 Chronicles

18:14   **69**

Psalms

35:10   **67**
82:3   **21, 28**
146:5–9   **67**

Proverbs

16:11   **11, 21**
16:12   **69**
20:7   **21, 28**
29:4   **69**
29:14   **69**

Isaiah

10:1–3   **69**
26:7   **21, 28**
chap 58   **68**

Jeremiah

9:24   **21, 28**
22:1–5   **68**
22:15–16   **32**

Job

29:14–17   **21, 28**

Ezekiel

18:5   **20, 28**
18:7   **20**
34:16–24   **31–32**

Amos

8:4–8   **67**

Micah

3:1–4   **67**
6:6–8   **68**
6:8   **21, 28**

Zechariah

7:9–12   **67**

Matthew

5:43–48   **71**
6:25–30   **70**
22:34–40   **71**
25:31–46   **68, 72**

Luke

10:25–37   **72**

Acts

2:42–47   **71**
4:32–35   **71**

Romans

13:1–7   **69**

1 Corinthians

chap 13   **72**

2 Corinthians

9:8–10   **21, 28**

Ephesians

4:28   **62, 71**

Colossians

1:16–20   **70**
4:1   **21**

1 Thessalonians

4:11–12   **62**

2 Thessalonians

3:6–10   **71**
3:6–8   **62**
3:10–12   **62**

Hebrews

1:1–4   **70**

1 Peter

2:13–17   **69**

1 John

3:11–24   **72**

Index of Authors

Member Institutions of the Christian College Coalition

Anderson College
Anderson, IN 46012

Asbury College
Wilmore, KY 40390

Azusa Pacific University
Azusa, CA 91702

Bartlesville Wesleyan
College
Bartlesville, OK 74003

Belhaven College
Jackson, MS 39202

Bethany Nazarene
College
Bethany, OK 73008

Bethel College
Mishawaka, IN 46545

Bethel College
North Newton, KS
67117

Bethel College
3900 Bethel Drive
St. Paul, MN 55112

Biola University
13800 Biola Avenue
La Mirada, CA 90639

Bryan College
Dayton, TN 37321

Calvin College
Grand Rapids, MI
49506

Campbell University
Buies Creek, NC 27506

Campbellsville College
Campbellsville, KY
42718

Central Wesleyan
College
Central, SC 29630

Colorado Christian
College
Lakewood, CO 80226

Covenant College
Lookout Mountain, TN
37350

Dallas Baptist
Dallas, TX 75211

Dordt College
Sioux Center, IA 51250

Eastern College
St. Davids, PA 19087

Eastern Mennonite
College
Harrisonburg, VA 22801

Eastern Nazarene
College
23 E. Elm Avenue
Quincy, MA 02170

Evangel College
Springfield, MO 65802

Fresno Pacific College
Fresno, CA 93702

Geneva College
Beaver Falls, PA 15010

George Fox College
Newberg, OR 97132

Gordon College
Wenham, MA 01984

Goshen College
Goshen, IN 46526

Grace College
200 Seminary Drive
Winona Lake, IN 46590

Grand Canyon College
P.O. Box 11097
Phoenix, AZ 85061

Greenville College
Greenville, IL 62246

Houghton College
Houghton, NY 14744

Huntington College
Huntington, IN 46750

John Brown University
Siloam Springs, AR
72761

Judson College
Elgin, IL 60120

King College
Bristol, TN 37620

The King's College
Briarcliff Manor, NY
10510

Lee College
Cleveland, TN 37311

LeTourneau College
Longview, TX 75607

Malone College
Canton, OH 44709

Marion College
Marion, IN 46952

The Master's College
Newhall, CA 91322

Messiah College
Grantham, PA 17027

Mid-America Nazarene
College
Olathe, KS 66061

Milligan College
Milligan College, TN
37682

Mississippi College
Clinton, MS 39058

Mount Vernon
Nazarene College
Mt. Vernon, OH 43050

North Park College
5125 North Spaulding
Avenue
Chicago, IL 60625

Northwest Christian
College
11th and Alder
Eugene, OR 97401

Northwest Nazarene
College
Nampa, ID 83651

Northwestern College
Orange City, IA 51041

Northwestern College
3003 Snelling N.
Roseville, MN 55113

Nyack College
Nyack, NY 10960

Olivet Nazarene College
Kankakee, IL 60901

Oral Roberts University
7777 South Lewis
Tulsa, OK 74171

Palm Beach Atlantic
College
1101 South Olive
Avenue
West Palm Beach, FL
33401

Point Loma Nazarene
College
3900 Lomaland Drive
San Diego, CA 92106

Roberts Wesleyan
College
2301 Westside Drive
Rochester, NY 14624

Seattle Pacific
University
Seattle, WA 98119

Simpson College
San Francisco, CA
94134

Sioux Falls College
Sioux Falls, SD 57101

Southern California
College
55 Fair Drive
Costa Mesa, CA 92626

Spring Arbor College
Spring Arbor, MI 49283

Sterling College
Sterling, KS 67579

Tabor College
Hillsboro, KS 67063

Taylor University
Upland, IN 46989

Trevecca Nazarene
College
333 Murfreesboro Road
Nashville, TN 37210

Trinity College
2077 Half Day Road
Deerfield, IL 60015

Trinity Christian College
6601 West College Drive
Palos Heights, IL 60463

Warner Pacific College
2219 Southeast 68th
Avenue
Portland, OR 97215

Warner Southern
College
Lake Wales, FL 33853

Westmont College
955 La Paz Road
Santa Barbara, CA
93108

Wheaton College
Wheaton, IL 60187

Whitworth College
Spokane, WA 99251